A history of the town of Berkeley, its church, castle etc., etc.

Fisher, John, curate of Berkeley (Eng.)
4n

Nabu Public Domain Reprints:

You are holding a reproduction of an original work published before 1923 that is in the public domain in the United States of America, and possibly other countries. You may freely copy and distribute this work as no entity (individual or corporate) has a copyright on the body of the work. This book may contain prior copyright references, and library stamps (as most of these works were scanned from library copies). These have been scanned and retained as part of the historical artifact.

This book may have occasional imperfections such as missing or blurred pages, poor pictures, errant marks, etc. that were either part of the original artifact, or were introduced by the scanning process. We believe this work is culturally important, and despite the imperfections, have elected to bring it back into print as part of our continuing commitment to the preservation of printed works worldwide. We appreciate your understanding of the imperfections in the preservation process, and hope you enjoy this valuable book.

HISTORY
OF THE
TOWN OF BERKELEY,
CHURCH, CASTLE,
ETC., ETC.,

BY THE REV. JOHN FISHER,
LEICESTER,
(Formerly Curate of Berkeley)
Author of the "History of Burgh, Lincolnshire."

Second Edition, corrected and enlarged.

LONDON: HOULSTON & WRIGHT,
65, PATERNOSTER ROW;
LEICESTER: T. CHAPMAN BROWNE, BIBLE AND CROWN
1864.

"A painful work it is, I'll assure you, wherein what toyle hath been taken, as no man thinketh, so no man believeth, but he that hath made the trial."

Ant. A. Wood.

TO

THE RIGHT HON.

𝔖𝔦𝔯 𝔐𝔞𝔲𝔯𝔦𝔠𝔢-𝔉𝔯𝔢𝔡𝔢𝔯𝔦𝔠𝔨-𝔉𝔦𝔱𝔷𝔥𝔞𝔯𝔡𝔦𝔫𝔤𝔢 𝔅𝔢𝔯𝔨𝔢𝔩𝔢𝔶,

G.C.B.,

BARON FITZHARDINGE,

ADMIRAL, R.N.,

A PRIVY COUNCILLOR,

OF BERKELEY CASTLE, IN THE COUNTY OF GLOUCESTER;

AND A MAGISTRATE FOR THE SAME COUNTY,

&c., &c., &c.,

𝔗𝔥𝔦𝔰 𝔙𝔬𝔩𝔲𝔪𝔢,

DESCRIPTIVE OF THE INTERESTING DOMAIN AND ANCIENT CASTLE

OF HIS ANCESTORS,

IS, BY PERMISSION, MOST RESPECTFULLY DEDICATED,

BY HIS LORDSHIP'S MOST HUMBLE

AND MOST OBEDIENT SERVANT,

THE AUTHOR.

INTRODUCTION

TO THE FIRST EDITION.

The Writer of the following pages is of opinion that as there are everywhere persons who have never taken the trouble to acquaint themselves with the history of the place of their abode, a popular HISTORY OF BERKELEY may not be unacceptable.

The want of such a Work has long been complained of; and it appeared to the Author that if he could present in a cheap and accessible volume all the information necessary for a good Guide Book, he would acceptably supply that desideratum.

He was unwilling, indeed, that a Town possessed of so many historical associations, and containing objects of great antiquarian interest, and much picturesque beauty, should not have its *special* monograph, while many Towns of inferior note have their elaborate Histories.

If this little Work tend to increase the interest of the inhabitants of *Berkeley* in all that concerns their ancient Town, or if it serve as a Guide to the many occasional visitors of the locality, the Author's object will have been attained.

BERKELEY, MAY, 1856.

INTRODUCTION

TO THE

SECOND EDITION.

In this Edition, several errors in the first are corrected, and many omissions supplied.

The whole Work has undergone a careful revisal, and the Author hopes it is thereby rendered more worthy of the reception which the Public have already kindly given to it.

LEICESTER, June, 1804.

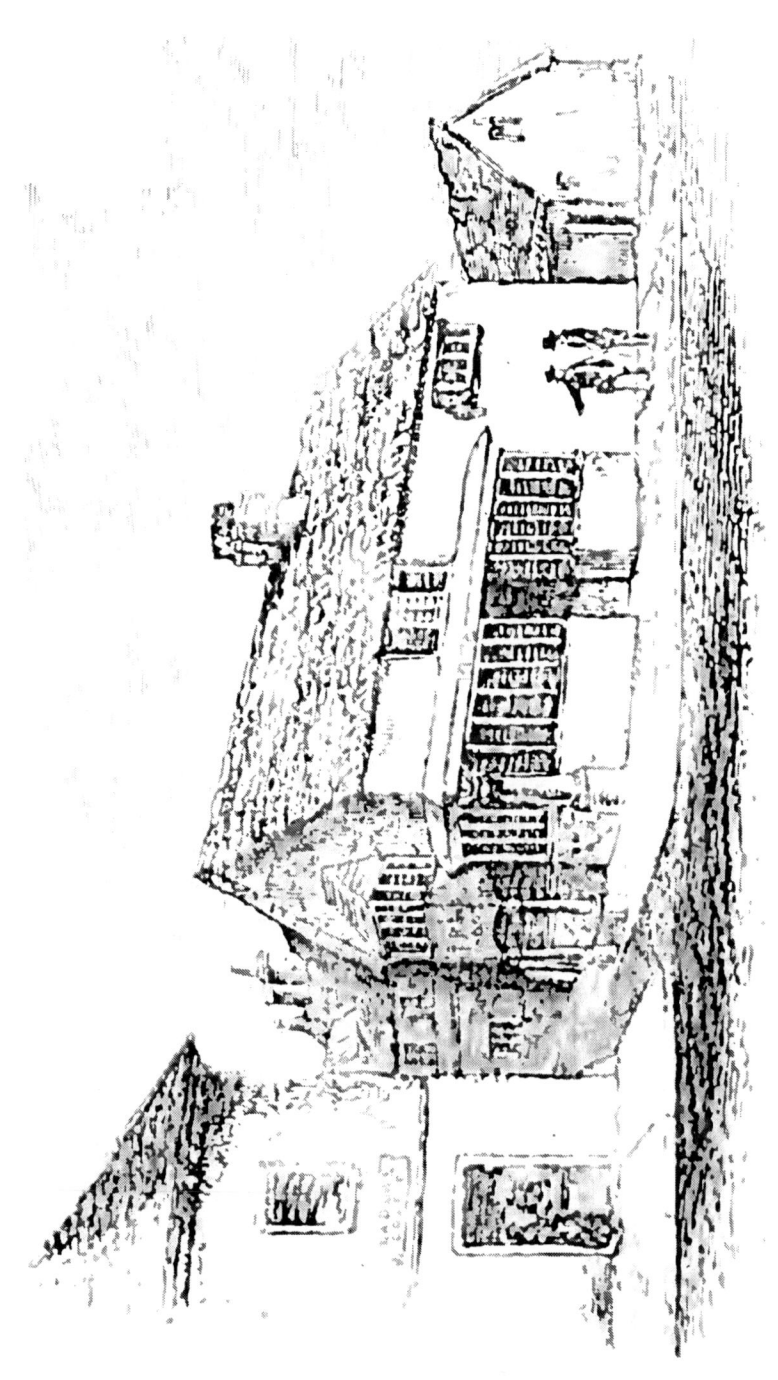

HISTORY
OF THE
TOWN OF BERKELEY.

CHAPTER I.

THE TOWN.

"Berkeley, whose fair seat hath been famous long," as Drayton in his "Polyolbion" hath it, is an ancient Borough and Market-town in the hundred of Berkeley, Gloucestershire, but sends no member to Parliament. It is the largest parish in the county, and gives name to the greatest division, for taking in the tithings it is twenty-four miles in compass.

There are seven considerable hamlets, or tithings, in this parish, viz.:

1. The Borough of Berkeley.
2. Alkington, which contains Swanley, Woodford, Rugbagge, Michaelwood Chase, Wick, and Newport.
3. Bradstone, now called Breadstone, which gave name to a family who were the ancient lords of it.
4. Hinton, anciently called Seven-Hams, and part of Halmore.

5. Hamfallow, in which are Ma... ...part of Ha'more.

6. Ham, in which are C...ton, B... ...Wh... Par..., Peddington, and N.w Pa.k.

7. Stone, which ha. a Ch.pel d... ...to A Saint.

Th. .wn i. .ix..n .il. south ... .G. ..., b.. w... ...d .. .n Durley, ...om Thornbur., and ...he ea.tward ...... t.. .. Severn, with which there i. a navigal.l. c... .... .y means of a narrow ch.nne. cal.ed .h. P.

It i. plea.antly .itu...'.on an emi.... , ...rounded b. ..c. m..... ...d., w..h ... ...ar... ..rly noted for the pr....... in .t... ... ...

The .il is com,.... .f .... clay an. ....

T... .rigin .of .h. n.me .f .ny . ...rth ..kin. f.r, .. it will of... .n .h. .. .. .i.tory.

B... ..., in the Saxon ... .e B... ..., ...r' B... ..., deriv.. it nare b... B..., .. t..... ...., .d L... L..., w...h .. .. L... h-t.. g. w. . .. p.... ... ...m. .

I. .q .. .. w.. , ...C.. ...g ... . wi.. ....d W... ...M.. "B... ... ... S... ... ...j and ... . h... .. . w.. N..... . I.. . N. ... ... " N.. .. . N.

The founder is unknown, but the account of its dissolution is remarkable, and the Author here abbreviates it from the page of Walter de Mape:—

Godwin, Earl of Kent, the father of Harold, whose daughter Editha was married to Edward the Confessor, was a deep designing man, who would stop at no crime which promised to increase his worldly good. This nobleman had engrossed all power in the reign of Edward the Confessor, and held possession of many great estates. He cast his eye on this fruitful Manor, and being a man most deeply practised in devising how to do injury, obtained possession of this place by leaving, as he passed this way, his Nephew, a beautiful young man (pretending that he was sickly) in the Nunnery here until he returned back, and instructed him how to effect its destruction. By fair speech and presents said youth seduced the Abbess and most of the nuns, and informing his uncle thereof, the Earl reported this conquest to the King, who, finding all that was told him to be true, thrust out the Nuns, destroyed the Nunnery, and gave Berkeley to Godwin, who settled it upon his Grandson; but he refused to eat anything that came off this Manor, because of the destruction of the Abbey; and the ......
.... Uncestre W...... for her ......
..... b.... a Ber....., ...t... De...
ly B..... bal G.t.

to squander away any part of this Manor because of the destruction of the Abbey."

The wickedness of this Earl Godwin did not long prosper, for he died in the Easter of 1053, and his eldest son, Harold, succeeded to his territories and command, and to even more than Godwin's authority in the nation.

The following is a translation of an account of Berkeley in Domesday Book,* where it is styled a royal demesne, and is thus described:—"In Berkeley King Edward had five hides; and in the demesne two ploughs; and twenty villanes and five bordars with eleven ploughs, and nine bondmen;† and seven [...] twelve shillings."

---

* Domesday Book. When King Alfred divided [...] Counties, Hundreds, and Tithings, [...] an Inquest [...] several districts and digested into a Register called Domesday Book, the judicial or judgment book, reposed in the church of [...] thence called Doomsday Book [...] which King Edward [...] to refer in the first chapter of [...]

The general survey taken by King William the Conqueror [...] the precedent of King Alfred's [...] at a [...] an addition to, the same name, [...] into Domesday Book. And therefore a trifling derivation [...] the name [...] called from the church where it was first reposed. Nor [...] wiser conjecture to ascribe it to [...] When the appellation doth read, it [...] or register from which sentence and [...] of estates: whence [...] Latin writers commonly called [...]

† Bondmen, per [...] household [...] distinct from the Villanes, who were the [...]

The Bordars were Cottagers, from the Anglo-Saxon [...]

"There are ten tadeshoure tre, having seven hi e, and seven ploug s.

"There is a Ma k t Place (Forum) in wh ch teen vassa's dwell, and they p y tax e or rent (reasant cenrus in firma)."

Thus at thi period King Edward held 1,44   , thirty-four tenants, and two mill for h wn   .

Ten f emen held 1,400 acre ; and   ent   e men re ed in the t wn.

According to D m day the foll g ham' longed to Berc ela :—

HAMLETS.	HIDE .	
In Hill	4	
,, Alkinton	4	64
,, Hinton	4	6
,, C m	17	272
,, G ssington	4	64
,, D rsley	3	48
,, Cowley	4	64
,, U ey	2	32
,, Nimpsfield	3	4
,, Wotton	15 nd ½ a v r	24
,, Sim n t l	6½	
,, Kir	4	
,, B v a	10	1
,, O t		8
,, Alm n ry	2	32
,, H rf l	8	1
,, W t n	7 nd 1 virg	11
,, E n	5	8
,, Cr all	2	
,, A ingh m	9	1
,, A l orth	3	1
	111 nt 1½	1 9 5

It must be observed here, that the Domesday Record only specified lands under arable cultivation; meadows and pastures being then held in common, and not reckoned. The above hamlets are therefore estimated far below their contents.

In these there were, in King Edward's time, 1,960 acres (49½ plough tillages) held in the king's own hands; and 5,040 acres (126 plough tillages) held by 242 farmers, and 142 cottagers, paying services instead of rent, and rendering poultry, eggs, &c.

There were 127 serfs, living at the discretion of the lord. Nineteen freemen held 1,920 acres. There were twenty-two soccage tenants, and fifteen female serfs, dependent entirely upon the lord.

There were eight mills at rather more than seven shillings a year rent each.

This information presents a vast fund for the investigation of the Antiquary, and even the non-calculating mind cannot fail to be aware of the extent of this immense Manor.*

On the death of Edward the Confessor, Jan. 5th, 1065, Harold, eldest son of the deceased Earl Godwin, was proclaimed king, but was killed at the battle of Hastings, October 14th, 1066, when William the Conqueror obtained the victory, and became king of England.

* Agriculture at that early period was an employment for mere maintenance—not as at present, for the exercise of science and the investment of capital.

William now bestows the Manor of Berkeley upon Roger, Lord of Dursley and of its castle, who thereupon takes the name of Roger de Berkeley. This Roger was a great benefactor to the priory of Stanley St. Leonards, and in 1091 became a shorn monk therein. Having no issue, this Manor descended to his Nephew and heir William de Berkeley, Lord of Dursley, and founder of the Abbey of Kingswood in 1139.

He was succeeded by his eldest son and heir, Roger de Berkeley, Lord of Dursley. This Roger held his lands *in capite*, at a yearly rent of £500. 17s. 2d. to the Crown. He was deprived of his Manors of Dursley and Berkeley for taking part with Stephen against Henry II.; but King Henry being intreated by the Lords of his realm, restored the Barony and Manor of Dursley to him for his own inheritance; and gave the Barony and Manor of Berkeley to Robert Fitzharding, the son of Harding, the King of Denmark's son, for his eminent services and fidelity. This extensive Manor is still vested in his posterity, the present noble Baron Fitzhardinge being descended from him. Before taking leave, for the present, of this Barony and Manor, the author would observe, that they were alienated to King Henry VII. and his heirs male, by William Berkeley, seventh Lord, and Marquess of Berkeley; but upon the death of King Edward VI., the last heir male of Henry VII., Henry Berkeley, twelfth Lord by right, succeeded as heir to the seventh Lord to Berkeley

Castle and lands, and thus recovered the ancient honor and precedency of the family.

> "'Describe the Borough,'—though our idle tribe
> May love description, can we so describe,
> That you shall fairly streets and buildings trace,
> And all that gives distinction to a place?"
> *Crabbe.* "The Borough," Letter I.

Though the town may in general be considered as irregularly built, yet there are a few good houses in it; it consists of these streets,—High Street, Salter Street, Marybrook* Street alias Madbrook Street, and Canonbury street alias Spurryers Street, and the Stock Lane. It was anciently distinguished by monuments of antiquity, viz.:—On the right of the road, entering the town from Gloucester, stood Longbridge Hospital, founded by the first Maurice de Berkeley,† long since gone to ruins, and of which there are no traces left. The site is now green meadows: "Ipsæ periere ruinæ." At the junction of the four streets stood the Market Cross, and in High Street there was a cross opposite the west window of the church, of which not a trace is left; near Lockfast Bridge was an ancient water mill, spoken of in Domesday and also mentioned in the twelfth century, where the corn of the castle was ground: in Salter Street, near the Market Cross, stood the old Market House, a very ancient and curious

---

* St. Mary's Brook was a reputed mineral spring, much valued by the ancient inhabitants.

† In the reign of King Henry II.

building, forming an archway over the causeway, and extending into the street. It was pulled down rather more than sixty-eight years ago.

There were several antique houses in the Market Place, but these are long since decayed.

A few mean specimens, however, of ancient architecture still remain in the town, but most of the old houses have been re-fronted and repaired either during the last century or recently.

Berkeley is an ancient Corporate town, being incorporated by prescription from the Earls of Berkeley by the style of "the Burgesses and Merchants of Berkeley, their heirs and assigns," about the 20th, and again in the 46th of Henry III. It is under the government of a Mayor (who is only titular, and is sworn at the Court-Leet of the Earl of Berkeley), and twelve Aldermen who have been Mayors; but their privilege is merely nominal, though the forms of a Corporation are continued to this day. It never sent any Member to Parliament. Leland, who wrote in 1520, says of it—

"The Towne of Berkeley is no great thinge, but it standythe well, and in a very good soyle.

"It hathe very muche occupied, and yet somewhat dothe, Clothing.

"The Churche stondithe on an Hille at the South Ende of the Towne.

"And the Castle stondithe at the South West ende of the Churche.

"It is no great thinge.

"Divers Towres be in the compase of it.

"The Warde of the first Gate is mitely stronge, and a Bridge over a Dyche to it. There is a Sqware Dongeon Towre in the Castle, *sed non stat in mole egestæ Terræ.*

"There longe to Berkeley four Parks, two Chases. Okely Parke, hard by. Whitwike. New Parke. Hawlle Parke. Miche Wood Chase."*

However affairs may have gone of old, the inhabitants may be said at this day to have *nomen sine re*, and may rather boast of the glories of the feudal ages than pride themselves on having any present municipal *status*.

At a short distance from the town flows the little river Avon, on the banks of which during the summer months many a juvenile Izaak Walton may generally be seen; it soon enters the Pill, and hence into the Severn.

The little Avon takes its rise at Boxwell, a parish above Wotton-under-Edge, nearly nine miles up the country; this village derives its name from a large Box-tree wood, where is a well which sends out this stream.

There was not any Fair here until Thomas Lord Berkeley, fourth of that name, obtained a grant in the 18th year of King Richard II., 1394, to have one held yearly on the vigil and the day of the Invention

* Leland's Itin., v. 7, p. 96.

of Holy Cross, called Holy Rood Day (May 3rd). This Fair continues to this day, but since the new style of chronology was introduced into Great Britain (1752), it has been held on the 14th.* There is also another Annual Fair, held the second Monday in December; it was instituted about twenty-five years ago by the late Mr. Alfred Pearce, Wine and Spirit Merchant, of this town.

And there is an Annual Market, called the Great Market, held the first Tuesday in November.

A Monthly Market was established February 2nd, 1859, for Cattle, Cheese, &c.; on which occasion ninety gentlemen and farmers sat down to dinner at the Berkeley Arms Hotel, Colonel Berkeley, M.P., Chairman.

POPULATION.

The following is an extract from the Population Tables:—

Borough of Berkeley.

	1801	1811	1821	1831	1841	1851	1861
Total....	658	616	838	901	926	949	1012
Males....	330	296	330	423	412	424	465

THE CANAL.

The Gloucester and Berkeley Canal was commenced in the year 1794, and completed in 1827, at a cost of

---

* The earlier Lords of Berkeley would not have Fairs held in the town, being unwilling that a multitude of people should be assembled so near their Castle, and thus endanger a surprise from the enemy in those agitated times. They purchased charters for Fairs to be held at Wotton, Dursley, Newport, and Cambridge, in this hundred of Berkeley.

£500,000. It begins in the Severn at Sharpness Point, about three miles north of Berkeley, and terminates at Gloucester in spacious docks, the distance being only sixteen and a half miles.

Vessels of eight hundred tons burden are enabled to reach Gloucester by this canal, whereas by the Severn the distance is about thirty miles with a difficult and hazardous navigation.

THE DISSENTERS.

The Dissenters from the strict doctrines of the Church of England form collectively in this town a small portion of the community, and two Chapels have been erected by them.

The denominations are Wesleyans and Independents. The former, having formed themselves into a congregation, built a Chapel on Canonbury Hill, in the year 1805; and the latter erected their Chapel in Salter Street, in the year 1835. The pew-rent principle is not adopted here, either in support of the Chapel or Preacher; but voluntary contributions are given for those purposes. Sunday schools have been established in connection with these Chapels.

BERKELEY CHURCH.—North-west View.

Chapter II.

THE CHURCH, &c.

In a country town the Church is generally the first attraction for a stranger. Even to those who are not Antiquarians, the examination of such edifices is always pleasant and gratifying, especially when the mind is impressed with the fact that they were raised by the labours of our forefathers. Our ancient churches have received a greater share of the munificence, talents, and labours of our forefathers than most other buildings. In them we find such testimonies of piety, such traces of simple trustfulness, such hopefulness:—

> "The place is purified with hope,
> The hope that is of prayer;
> And human love, and heavenward thought,
> And pious faith are there."

According to the "Cartularium de Reading," the church of Berkeley, with the Prebend annexed, and the Prebend of the Nuns, was given by Adelida, the

Queen and second wife of Henry I., to the Monks of Reading.

Dugdale, in his "Monasticon," says;—"This donation was further confirmed by the Empress Maude," daughter of the said King Henry I. And in the Manuscripts of Dr. Parsons, at Oxford, it is said, that "There was an ancient church, dedicated to our Saviour and His Saints, upon whose wall was written the Apocalypse in Latin. It was joined to the old tower." Upon the alienation of the Advowson, an agreement was made, during the reign of Henry II., between the Canons of St. Augustine, Bristol, and the Monks of Reading, concerning the church of Berkeley, to which there were subordinate chapels, by paying to the latter twenty marks. Thus we see that there formerly stood in the churchyard a tower, to which a church was joined; and, it is to be observed, that this old church was not so much a Parochial as a Collegiate or Prebendal church. The Abbeys, by means of the Pope, having quashed this Collegiate church, Robert Fitzharding proceeded to erect the present edifice, at some distance from the other, which accounts for the estrangement of the tower. Smyth says, " The Church and Advowson of this Parish with its Chapels was, by Robert, the sonne of Harding, the first Lord Berkeley, in the time of Kinge Henry Seconde, given amongst others to the Monastery of St. Augustine, Bristol, at his first foundation thereof; which the Abbots of the Convent shortly after found means, with the Bishop of

Worcester, and an Incumbent of their own presentinge, to appropriate with others." And again he says, "The appropriation of the Church, as also the Vicaridge, which it presented to, belongs (as in Mr. Smyth's time it did) to the Dean and Chapter of Bristol, of newe erected in 38 Henry VIII., of which church the blessed Virgin Mary was the tutelary Saint, to whom the same was dedicated."

The Records in the Tower of London show, that "the Lords of the Manor anciently used to pay Peter's pence* to the Bishop of Worcester, 16s. 4d. yearly, and hee the same to the Bishop of Rome; which, being unpaid for certaine yeares, by reason their lands came into the hands of Edward II., on account of the rebellion of Maurice Lord Berkeley, the Bishop was restored to have them paid unto him, as anciently he had."—*Claus.* 16 *Edward II. m.* 22. *F.*

The Rectory, after the Dissolution of Monasteries, formed part of the endowment of the Chapter of Bristol, but "was sold during the grand rebellion."—*Harl. MS.* 5013.

At the Restoration it reverted to the Chapter, in whom it still remains.

Bigland says, page 153:—"The Benefice is a Vicarage, in the presentation of the Earl of Berkeley, the

* Peter's pence were alms which the Kings of England had very long been accustomed to pay to the See of Rome; but in 1533, it was enacted that this imposition should be done away with.—*Act* 25 *Henry VIII.*, c. 20.

Chapter of Bristol having alienated their right, by Act of Parliament, to George first Earl of Berkeley, in consideration of an exchange of the Advowsons of Berkeley and Hinton for that of Sutton Bonnington, in the county of Nottingham. But the *impropriation* * is retained by them."

The Benefice is a Vicarage, in the Deanery of Dursley, of which the Earl of Berkeley is Patron, valued *now* at £750 a-year. The Rectorial tithe, amounting to £1,735 a-year and upwards, goes to the Dean and Chapter of Bristol, or their Lessees.

The Rev. John Seton-Karr was presented to the Benefice in 1839, by the Right Honourable Baron Segrave, afterwards Earl Fitzhardinge; but the Earl of Berkeley was *then*, and is *now*, the Patron.

The Church, dedicated to the Blessed Virgin Mary, is a large and handsome structure, consisting of a nave, two aisles, and a chancel.

It is considered by Antiquarians to be by far the finest in its own neighbourhood.

It was new pewed in the year 1732.

The style of architecture is the early English, very pure and good; and if Robert Fitzharding were the founder of the present church, it is evident that the

---

* At the dissolution of Monasteries, A.D. 1537, certain Livings were disposed of to the best bidders, or to the greatest favourites, and so became Lay property; these are called *Impropriations*. *Appropriations* are such as were appointed to the erecting or augmenting of some Bishopric, Deanery, or religious foundation.

whole building must have been reconstructed from its first form, by gradual reparations.

A movement for the repairs and restoration of the church is *now* in progress, and about £1,400 have already been subscribed; but £1,000 more are wanted.

The building is so completely plastered and whitewashed within and without, that the masonry is hid.

The Author must, therefore, confine himself to the present appearance and architectural character of the edifice.

West Front.

Externally.—This doorway is set in a gable, between two blank pointed arches, and has a very obtuse arch elaborately foliated and resting on detached shafts with flowered capitals.

It is low—doorways being intentionally made *low*, in order to teach humility.

This end is flanked by two large buttresses, the northern one having a staircase somewhat curiously attached, the southern one was a few years ago very feebly repaired.

These terminations to the northern and southern aisles are mere botches, and underwent repairs in the year 1818; had towers been built, the termination would have been of the most striking character.

The window above is a quintuplet of five round-headed lancets trefoiled, with banded shafts and floriated capitals to each.

whole building must have been reconstructed from its first form, by gradual reparations.

A movement for the repairs and restoration of the church is *now* in progress, and about £1,400 have already been subscribed; but £1,000 more are wanted.

The building is so completely plastered and whitewashed within and without, that the masonry is hid.

The Author must, therefore, confine himself to the present appearance and architectural character of the edifice.

West Front.

Externally.—This doorway is set in a gable, between two blank pointed arches, and has a very obtuse arch elaborately foliated and resting on detached shafts with flowered capitals.

It is low—doorways being intentionally made *low*, in order to teach humility.

This end is flanked by two large buttresses, the northern one having a staircase somewhat curiously attached, the southern one was a few years ago very feebly repaired.

These terminations to the northern and southern aisles are mere botches, and underwent repairs in the year 1818; had towers been built, the termination would have been of the most striking character.

The window above is a quintuplet of five round-headed lancets trefoiled, with banded shafts and floriated capitals to each.

They increase in height towards the centre, and there is also a correspondent increase in point of width. The roof-pitch of the nave has evidently been lowered.

These portions are early English.

Internally.—The doorway has a segmental head, having a label and a moulded jamb, and is flanked by a blank pointed arch on each side, answering to those of the exterior.

In each arch there is a tablet, one to the memory of Sidney, the other to that of Joyner-Ellis.

The quintuplet window above assumes internally the form of one large window, the whole being grouped under a bold semi-circular arch rising from detached banded shafts.

The effect is fine and imposing.

In the year 1732 a gallery was first erected, but in 1794 the present one was built instead thereof, and the Organ was then removed thither from the rood-screen in the chancel: thus this beautiful window and doorway are partially concealed.

On the front of the gallery is a painting of St. Cæcilia. She was a Roman lady, and lived in the year of our Lord 225. Tradition relates that she was so skilful a musician, that an angel who visited her was drawn down from the mansions of the blessed by the charms of her melody; to which circumstance Dryden alludes in the conclusion of his celebrated "Ode to Cæcilia."

The following is a copy of a printed bill in the possession of Mr. John Croome, of Berkeley, who kindly favoured the Author with it:—

"*Berkeley, Saturday, October 8th,* 1791.

It having been intimated that some of the subscribers to the Organ have expressed a wish to hear the Instrument previous to the public opening of it on Tuesday next, the Rev. Mr. Hupsman, considering himself particularly obliged to them for their liberal contributions, and ever solicitous to obtain and to preserve the good will of his parishioners, has given the Organist such directions for the service of to-morrow, both in the morning and evening, as he hopes will give general satisfaction.

N.B.—Should this notice be omitted to be delivered to any subscriber, it is requested to be placed to the account of accident, not of neglect."

The following is a copy of a letter entered in the book for the Tything of Alkington:—

"*White Hart, Berkeley, April* 10*th,* 1792.

Sir,—I am requested to inform you that the Churchwardens and Gentlemen of this Parish composing this meeting, feel themselves infinitely obliged to you for the assistance of your pencil, which contributes so much to adorn the front of the Organ Gallery. And farther I am desired to say, that the beauty of the Painting receives additional taste from the very handsome manner in which you have presented it.

And that posterity may know to whom they are indebted, I have received directions to record the same in the parish books.

In the name, and at the request of the meeting, I subscribe myself, Sir,

Your much obliged and obedient Servant,

JOHN CLARK."

"To Mr. Edward Pearce,
    Middlemills."

The visitor entering the church at the western portal finds himself in

The Nave,

which is spacious, arcades of unusual beauty forming a view terminated at the east end by a lofty chancel arch with a stone roodscreen across it. It is 96 feet long by 27 feet 3 inches wide. It was slightly repaired in the year 1834-5.

The nave itself is early English.

There are seven arches on each side, of the most perfect proportion.

The mouldings are very singular; and the label terminations are all heads, with different head dresses.

The twelve clustered pillars, which support these beautiful arches, have many peculiarities; a Bloxam or a Scott would do that justice to them which the Author feels himself unequal to do. He would, however, observe that all the capitals, except one of these pillars, are similar, being floriated; the one on the south side, instead of floriation, has a mere round capital with nail-heads set at distances from each other. The label-termination over this non-floriated capital has the grotesque device of a frog knocking two human heads together.

The space above the arches is unusually high, and the north side having no clerestory windows is most unpleasingly bare.

Even on the south side the clerestory windows, one

over each arch, are very short and broad round-headed trefoil lancets, with a deep but not wide internal splay and a label over. They want both height and width for the space which they occupy. A single label runs through the whole early English portion.

The roof is a low-pitched wooden one of Perpendicular date, and is a fair piece of workmanship. The corbels, on which it rests, are in form that of half a capital, supported by a head.

"In the great high wind of Nov. 26, 1703, the overflow of the Severn beat down the sea-wall, whereby the waters flowed above a mile over one part of the parish, and did great damage to the land. It carried away one house, which was by the sea-side, and a gentleman's stable, wherein was a horse, into the next ground. Twenty-six sheets of lead were blown off from the middle aisle* of the church, and taken up all joined together, as they were on the roof; the sheets weighing three hundred and a half one with another."
—*Rudder's Gloucestershire*, p. 270.

The Aisles.

The aisles, though of less beauty and importance than the other part of the church, contain two or three particulars worthy of notice.

They are chiefly of the Decorated style, and each contains six three-light windows of simple arch tracery foliated, of the same kind as those which terminate

* The Nave.

them to the west. That on the north side is shown to be of later date than the south aisle by the section of its label, and a slight difference in the tracery. The north aisle has no string course beneath its windows; the south has a roll externally.

The east window of the north aisle is unusually small and very high up in the wall, evidently to avoid interfering with the vestry. At the east end of the south aisle there are the remains of some decorated Sedilia, under a square-headed arch; these are coeval with the aisle. The window above them being shortened, and the external string course being lowered in proportion, are proofs of this.

The roofs of these aisles are of the same character as that of the nave. These aisles are each 96 feet long, the south one is $16\frac{1}{2}$ feet wide, but the north is only 15 feet wide.

The south entrance is a good specimen of Norman, but of a peculiar kind.

It is a square-headed doorway with an arch over it, and a heavy roll moulding going round the opening. The mouldings approach to the early English, but the capitals are of a local character.

Over this door is a beautiful little round window of geometrical and wheel tracery.

Round windows are a Gloucestershire localism, and are very common in churches in this county.

The buttresses on this south side are a tall and bold range without set-offs.

The north entrance is through a large porch, which was restored in the year 1810, the upper part of which is a modern parapet of the Perpendicular style; the lower portion, including the two doorways, is the Decorated.

The arch over the outer door is of the Ogee form, with mouldings and slender plain shafts; the inner one is plain, with wave moulding.

The vaulting is quadripartite of the same date, from corbels supported by heads.

The north and south aisles were repaired in the year 1834-5.

The church is less rich in monumental antiquities than probably would have been the case if it had not been a frequent custom with the ancient Lords of Berkeley to bury in their own foundation of St. Augustine's, Bristol. Still the array is curious and worthy of notice.

On the base of the second window of the south aisle are two cumbent figures, with a lamb couchant at the feet of each; and on the sill of the third window of this aisle there is a cumbent figure similar to, though longer than, the other two; these do not exceed a yard in length. They are called by Dr. Parsons, the children of Thomas Lord Berkeley, viz.:—Thomas, Maurice, and Edmund, who died in their infancy. But as these are habited as females, the Author begs leave to differ from this gentleman, and should say they were intended for Nuns.

Under the second arch, and opposite the above figures, on an altar-tomb, are the effigies of Thomas Lord Berkeley, and Catherine, his second wife, sculptured in white marble. Lord Berkeley is represented in the armour of the fourteenth century, charged with the family Coat of Arms, a mitre under his head, and a lion couchant at his feet; and the Lady with a head-dress of extraordinary shape and size, a cushion under her head, supported by an angel on each side, and a dog couchant at her feet. This Lord died in 1360, before which time the Nobles of this family were buried in St. Augustine's Abbey, Bristol. Some parts of the Lady's costume are worthy of notice. Over all she wears a mantle, under it a *supertunick* or *surceat*, surmounted by a corset, then newly invented, and an indication of her rank.*

On the wall of this aisle there are Tablets to the memories of the families of HICKES (emblazoned with Arms), JONES, JENKINS, RAYMOND, and HOOPER. At the west end of this aisle there is a very ancient square stone Font, for immersion, very capacious, and lined

---

* Strutt says, in his "Habits of the People of England," page 37, "Towards the conclusion of the fourteenth century the women were pleased with the appearance of a long waist; and in order to produce that effect, they invented a strange disguisement, called a *Corse* or *Corset*." Again he says, in page 376, "According to the Sumptuary Laws, made in the fourth year of King Edward IV., no woman under the degree of a Knight's wife or daughter might wear *wrought Corsets*." And by another clause in the same Act, "*Corsets worked with gold* were prohibited to all women under the rank of wife or daughter to a Lord." *Corse* is derived from the French *Corps*, a body; and so called because they covered the greater part of the body.

with lead. It is supported by four small shafts surrounding a large one; a form of the highest antiquity. It is enclosed with painted oak railings.

A sepulchral brass in the floor, on the south side of the Font, marks the resting-place of a Romish Priest.

The wall of the north aisle is occupied by tablets of benefactions, and a few *slabs to some of the parishioners.*

The following are copies of Benefactions:—

First Tablet.

Mr. JOHN ATWOOD of Berkeley in 1626 gave a Meadow called Longbridge to the poor of the Borough of Berkeley of the yearly value of £10. 10s.

Mr. THOMAS MACHIN of this parish in 1630 gave a ground lying near a meadow called *Parham* to the poor of this town of the yearly value of £3. 10s.

Mr. JOHN MALLETT of this parish in 1639 gave a ground lying near Prior's Wood three fifth parts to the poor of the Tything of Ham and two fifth parts to the poor of this town of the yearly value of £7. 10s.

The Bridewell House of Berkeley and a house called the Town House were given by an *unknown Benefactor* to the poor of this town and have been enjoyed by them time immemorial both together of the yearly value of £7. 10s.

The Tything Barn of Ham is charged with a payment to the poor of this town yearly 7s.

John Neale, Churchwarden, 1737.

Second Tablet.

Mr. THOMAS BAYLEY of this parish charged a ground called the Stunnings lying in Halmore with the payment to the poor of this town yearly 15s. and to the poor of the Tything of Hinton 15s.

Mr. RICHARD EVERETT of this parish gave the interest of £10 for ever to be paid to poor housekeepers of the Tything of Ham.

SAMUEL THURNER, M.B. of Magdalen Hall, Oxon, in 1696 gave lands lying part in the parish of Thornbury and part in the parish of Rockhampton for the teaching 26 boys of this town to read and write &c. of the yearly value of £15. 5s.

JOHN SMITH, A.M. of Magdalen Coll., Oxon, in 1717 gave a sum of money which with £40 given by the Right Honourable the Countess Dowager of Berkeley was laid out in lands in the parish of Berkeley for the teaching 12 boys three of this town and three of each Tything of the yearly value of £10. 10s.

John King, Churchwarden, 1737.

Third Tablet.

THOMAS HOPTON, Esq., in 1718 charged an estate lying in the parish of Littleton upon Severn in this county with the yearly payment of 30s. to the Minister of Berkeley and his successors for preaching two sermons one on Good Friday and the other on the 5th of November and 50s. yearly to the poor of this town

and the three Tythings in bread on the two aforesaid days.

Mrs. BRIDGET VICK of Berkeley in 1724 gave a ground called the Tyning lying in the Tything of Hinton* the profits whereof to be given in bread to the poor of the town and three Tythings on the 23rd of December of the yearly value of £4. 5s.

Mr. THOMAS PEARCE of Wick in this parish in 1728 charged an estate lying in Wick aforesaid with the payment of 12s. every Christmas Day to six poor men of the Tything of Alkington who regularly attend the Church and Sacrament.

John Greene, Churchwarden, 1737.

FOURTH TABLET.

Mrs. ELIZABETH BEVAN of Berkeley in 1728 gave in money £120 which her executor Mr. James Bevan laid out in lands and hath charged an estate called the Actrees lying near Berkeley Heath with the payment pursuant to the directions of the said Mrs. Bevan's will of £3 per annum to the Minister of Berkeley for reading prayers weekly and £3 yearly in bread to the poor of the town and three Tythings on the 23rd of December.

James Fords, Churchwarden, 1737

* The word Hinton ought to be Hamfallow.

Fifth Tablet.

Richard Tyler late of the City of Bristol Gent pursuant to the Will of his brother John Tyler Gent (both natives of this parish) in the year 1749 gave an estate situate in the Tything of Hinton for the following uses as appears by a deed enrolled in Chancery in the year 1750, viz.—thirty shillings to be equally divided between the clerk and the sexton of the parish Church of Berkeley for ringing the Bell and attending Divine Service as hereinafter directed. The remaining part of the yearly profits to be divided between the Ministers of Berkeley, Cam,* Wotton-under-edge, Cromhall, Tortworth, Dursley, and Thornbury, for reading morning prayer and preaching seventeen sermons annually in this Church on the following days and during Lent on the following subjects:—

1st—The Lent Fast.
2nd—Atheism and Infidelity.
3rd—The Catholic Church.
4th—Excellency of the Church of England.
5th—The defence of the Divinity of our Saviour.
6th—Baptism.
7th—Confirmation.
8th—Confession and Absolution.
9th—Errors of the Church of Rome.
10th—Enthusiasm and Superstition.
11th—Restitution.

* The word Cam ought to be Slimbridge.

12th—Attending Public Worship.
13th—Frequenting the Holy Communion.
14th—Repentance.

Sermons on the first seven subjects to be preached in the first year beginning on Ash-Wednesday 1750 and on the remaining other seven in the following year and so alternately and successively for ever. One of the said Sermons to be preached by each of the above-mentioned Ministers on every Wednesday in Lent four of the other ten by the Minister of Berkeley and the remaining six by the respective Ministers of the other Parishes aforesaid on the first Wednesday in every succeeding month within the compass of the year.*

---

* 14 Sermons to be preached in Lent, viz.:—

      7 one year beginning with 1750,
      7 the next year, and so on.
      ——
      14

    1 and 8 alternately by Berkeley;
    2 and 9 alternately by Slimbridge;
    And so on for ever.

Then, *i.e.*, after Lent, 4 Sermons by the Vicar of Berkeley, the first Wednesday in the month.

Then one Sermon the first Wednesday in the month by the other six Clergy.

Observe, the Lent Sermons will occupy the first Wednesdays in two of the months.

    7 Sermons in Lent, two of which will occupy the first Wednesdays in two months.
    4 by the Vicar of Berkeley.
    6 by the other Clergy.
    ——
    17 Sermons yearly.

Each Minister receives *now* thirty shillings every Wednesday.

Sixth Tablet.

John Harvey Ollney Lieutenant Colonel of the South Gloucester Militia by Will dated 3rd January 1836 gave to the town of Berkeley the sum of £300 to be paid in six months after the decease of his Wife and to be then invested in the names of the Vicar and Churchwarden the interest and annual produce to be laid out in the purchase of Coals and Blankets to be distributed at Christmas annually to such poor deserving persons in Berkeley as the Vicar and Churchwarden shall select. This Legacy became payable in July 1839 and was then invested in the purchase of £324. 6s. 6d. three per cent. consols which now stand in the joint names of

Rev. John Seton-Karr, Vicar.
Mr. Timothy Tratman, Churchwarden.

The other Tablets are to the memories of the families of Tratman, Pope, Pike, Bayley, Woollright, Smith, Davidge, Wiltshire, Joyner, Bailey, and Giles.

The Chancel.

The chancel arch before alluded to is remarkably lofty and very obtuse, like that at the west end; it is probably of the same date as the nave, with which it responds in some details.

The roodscreen across it is very beautiful in design. It is of stone, its style Perpendicular, with tracery

under a four-centred arch, the spandrils being open. It consists of three compartments; the lower part of the side ones in their original state no doubt was filled with solid panelling, and the central one closed with low doors; but all this has been removed.

On this beautiful screen are emblazoned 23 Coats of Arms, being the different alliances of the noble family of Berkeley.

Upon this screen the present organ was erected, in the year 1791, but was removed to where it now is in 1794, at a cost of £10.

The usual doorway to the rood-loft exists, and was approached on the north side by a staircase turret in the north aisle, now stopped up. The windows are irregular and of various kinds.

On the north side is a small lancet, and an early Decorated three-light window.

Below this last there are Decorated Sedilia, under a very elaborate and pointed arch.

The south side is lighted by three three-light Perpendicular windows; they were inserted in the year 1851, in the place of three others, one of which was a round window.

The great east window is a large Perpendicular one of nine lights under a four-centred arch, and was inserted in the year 1843, in the place of one of seven lights, and which matched the roodscreen. The roof is of the same character as that of the nave.

On the walls there are tablets, some of which are

emblazoned with Arms, to the families of Jenner, Weston, Pearce, Hopton, Gregory, Smith, Webb, and Morgan.

This chancel is 44 feet long and 25 wide.

The east end externally has diagonal buttresses, with small pinnacles on the set-offs, and an open pinnacle on the top of each buttress.

There are adjuncts on each side the chancel, a Vestry to the north, a Sepulchral Chapel of the Berkeleys to the south.

The *former* is of the Decorated period, and is entered by a doorway with a foliated arch, and retains a fair piece of workmanship in an ancient door. It has an old window, and outside there is a grand diagonal buttress.

The *latter* is the Perpendicular style, and rises from clustered shafts with round capitals of foliage.

Bloxam mentions this structure in his "Gothic Architecture."

It is divided into two parts, and is approached internally and externally.

Ceiling of the Ante-Chapel.

Centre compartment and central boss. Female Saint kneeling in prayer, with open book on a desk before her; above her, and eastward, the dove as emblem of the Holy Spirit.

The Berkeley knot in spandril of doorway.

In the Chapel.

First bay of the groining, lowermost boss over the door, upon which is an angel holding a shield, with the garments of our Saviour and of three disciples.

To the right, a monkey holding a bottle. Two cherubims with emblems of the crucifixion on shields— viz., cross, and spear, and reed; pillar and scourges.

At opposite corners—Fox in pulpit preaching to geese, and shepherds watching their flocks by night, with an angel above.

Four angels with musical instruments around central portion.

Central—the virgin with hands folded in prayer, and surrounded by cherubs; over her head, an angel holding a crown.

Opposite boss to that on which is the garments of our Saviour, another angel holding shield, with hammer, nails, and crown of thorns. *Central rib*—God the Father with the fingers uplifting two angels holding a riband, on which are the words, *Pater Noster*.

Below this to the south, on one of the bosses, is a mermaid with looking-glass and comb.

Compartment nearest Altar.

Four angels with scrolls, but no inscription to three of the bosses. Our Saviour in the centre, with the side pierced, and hands uplifted, surrounded by the emblems of the four evangelists.

Four bosses around, on which are a lamb, an eagle, an angel holding a scroll, and a beast with wings.

Under a low fretted arch is an altar-tomb of white marble, upon which recline two figures of an old* and young† man in armour; the Arms of Berkeley on the coats of mail, collars of a military order round both their necks; the mitre‡ under their heads, and a lion couchant under their feet.

The Arms on the chancel side are charged with *a file of three Lambeaux*, for Lord Thomas, the Grandson. On the side of the tomb within the chapel, are two rows of compartments of tabernacle work, containing figures of Knights, Ecclesiastics, and the Berkeley Arms enclosed within quartrefoils. This monument was erected for James, the sixth Lord Berkeley, and Thomas his Grandson.

On another altar-tomb of white marble are two cumbent figures; the man§ in armour with the mitre at his feet, and the woman in a court dress with a dog couchant at her feet, and a cushion under the head of each.

There are several marble Tablets, bearing inscriptions and arms to the Berkeley family.

This chapel was built about the year 1450. The exterior is richly embellished in the Gothic style, and

---

* James, Lord Berkeley, died October 22, 1463.
† Lord Thomas, his Grandson.
‡ The mitre is the crest of the Hardinges.
§ Henry, Lord Berkeley, died November 26, 1613,

has a very rich parapet adorned with the Tudor flower, not pierced, but employed as a sort of pannelling.

There are the same open pinnacles as at the east end, but of a richer sort, exhibiting in one case the figure of St. George subduing the Dragon. The windows externally have Ogee canopies.

The Author having now completed his description of Berkeley Church, it may not be uninteresting to many readers to know something about St. George and the Dragon.*

---

* This Saint suffered martyrdom for the sake of his religion, A.D. 290.

The legends relate several strange stories of him, which are so common they need not here be related. The Author will only give a short account how he came to be so much esteemed in England.

When Robert, Duke of Normandy, son of William the Conqueror, was fighting against the Turks, and laying siege to the famous City of Antioch, which was expected to be relieved by the Saracens, St. George appeared with an innumerable army coming down from the hills, all clad in white, with a red cross on his banner, to reinforce the Christians; this so terrified the Infidels, that they fled, and left the Christians in possession of the town.

This story made St. George extraordinarily famous in those times, and to be esteemed a patron, not only of the English, but of Christianity itself.

CHAPTER III.

THE CHURCHYARD.

"How many a bitter word 'twould hush,
 How many a pang 'twould save,
If life more precious held those ties
 Which sanctify the grave."---LANDON.

THE churchyard, where so many of

"The rude forefathers of the hamlet sleep,"

is a large piece of ground, and densely crowded with gravestones.

Among the epitaphs are the following singular ones:

DEAN SWIFT'S INSCRIPTION ON THE EARL OF SUFFOLK'S JESTER:—

"Here lies the Earl of Suffolk's Fool,
 Men called him Dicky Pearce;
His folly serv'd to make folks laugh,
 When wit and mirth were scarce.
Poor Dick, alas! is dead and gone;
 What signifies to cry?
Dickies enough are still behind,
 To laugh at by and by.
  Buried June 18, 1728, Aged 63 years."

This epitaph was composed by the celebrated Dean Swift, Chaplain to Charles, Earl of Berkeley; and was originally on a common head-stone, but the present altar-tomb was erected instead thereof in 1823.

"Here lyeth Thomas Peirce, whom no man taught,
 Yet he in Iron, Brasse, and Silver wrought;
He Jacks, and Clocks, and Watches (with art) made,
 And mended too when others' worke did fade.
Of Berkeley five tymes Mayor, this Artist was,
 And yet this Mayor, this Artist, was but grasse.
When his owne Watch was downe on the last day,
 He that made Watches, had not made a key
To winde it up, but uselesse it must lie,
 Until he rise againe no more to die.
   He deceased the 25 of Feb., 1665, Ætatis 77."

"Here lies a Woman by all the good esteem'd,
 Because they prov'd her really what she seem'd;
If thou wou'dst die as highly priz'd as she,
 Add to thy virtue true sincerity."

"How certain and uncertain is the life of man,
 Certain to die, but yet uncertain when;
In this we have an instance before our eyes,
 How soon a strong man sickens and he dies."

"Religion, honesty, and truth, ever by thee regarded:
Adorn'd thy life, O happy youth, thou'rt now in heaven rewarded."

"Pain was my portion,
Physick was my food,
Groans was my devotion,
Drugs did me no good;
Christ was my physician,
He knew which was best,
To ease me of my pain,
And take my soul to rest."

"Afflictions sore long time I bore,
Physicians were in vain;
Till Christ my Chief did give relief,
To ease me of my pain."

"Long night and day a bearing pain,
To wait for cure was all in vain;
In my prime, God thought it best,
To ease my pain and give me rest."

"All you that come my grave to see,
In dust I ly and so must thee,
Therefore take care, live righteous still,
Then welcome death come when it will."

"Rest gentle shade! in peaceful slumber lie,
Till the last trump proclaim salvation nigh;
Then joyful rise, shake off this cumbrous load,
Hail the bright morn! and prostrate hail thy God!"

"Wife and children, pray agree,
Serve the Lord and follow me;
My time is come, my days are spent,
The Lord did call and home I went."

"A tender Wife and Mother dear,
 A quiet neighbour resteth here."

"So brittle is the life of man,
 So soon it doth decay;
When all the glories of this world,
 Must pass and fade away.
The old must die we all agree,
 Likewise the young you plainly see;
Therefore prepare, make no delay,
 For no man knows the fatal day."

"Lord, when our stage of life is run,
 May we obtain the prize;
And like the daily setting sun,
 Go down again to rise."

"Farewell vain world, I've known enough of thee,
And now am careless what thou sayest of me;
Thy smiles I court not, nor thy frowns I fear,
My cares are past, my head lies quiet here;
What faults you've seen in me take care to shun,
And look at home, enough there's to be done."

"How swift the shuttle flies that weaves thy shroud."

"Remember me as you pass by,
 As you are now so once was I;
As I am now so you must be,
 Therefore prepare to follow me."

"Here lies a chaste and prudent wife,
Who in her lifetime hated strife;
A loving wife and tender mother,
'Tis hard to find out such another."

"Meek and gentle was her spirit,
Prudence did her life adorn;
Modest, she disclaimed all merit—
Tell me, am not I forlorn?
My body I to earth resign,
My soul to Providence divine."

"She took the cup to sip,
Too bitter was to drain;
She merely put it from her lip,
And went to sleep again."

"He was thy son—thine only son,
More dear than all beneath the sun:
Weep—if thy tears will give relief,
They may assuage a widow's grief;
Yet do not at his death repine,
But let the will of God be thine."

TO FIRST HUSBAND.

"Lo here in grave my husband dear is laid,
He was a loving father kind indeed;
So dear a friend so soon to lose 'tis hard,
But heaven to obtain is his reward."

TO SECOND HUSBAND.

"A Husband, a Father, and a Friend; a Father
To the Fatherless, and a Friend to the Widow."

"From a child brought up on the billow,
 His home was the fathomless deep;
But now the cold earth is his pillow,
 And sound and unbroken his sleep.
The winds and the waves cannot shake him;
 The tempest unheard shall arise,
Till the blast of the trumpet awake him;
 And call him in haste to the skies."

"High blustrous winds and lofty waves
 Have tossed me to and fro;
But now at least by God's decree,
 I harbour here below;
At anchor now I safely ride,
 For here I rest and sleep;
Once more again I must set sail,
 Our Saviour Christ to meet."

"Sweet Innocent too pure on Earth to stay,
 To bliss eternal thou hast led the way,
Oh! let us hope thy happiness to share,
 May thy angelic spirit guide us there.

Ere sin could blight or sorrow frown,
 Death came with friendly care,
The opening bud to heaven conveyed,
 And bade it blossom there."

"Stop Traveller! Oh! pause a moment here!
I crave no sigh! no sympathetic tear!
Nay pity not—thy tears forbear to shed:
They're vain—nay useless to th' unfeeling dead!
View but my fate! and thou wilt view thy own!
Time flies apace—thy days will soon be flown!

Reader! art thou prepar'd to die? Oh! say!
Art thou prepar'd to meet the judgment day?
Has thy past life been spent in joy and mirth?
Have thy past thoughts been solely bent on earth?
Ah! whence that sigh? does fear thy bosom fill?
Art thou then conscious of impending ill?
Reader! begone! Oh! tread that path I trod—
Pursue it—and thy soul prepare for God."

On an altar-tomb, near the north wall of the church, emblazoned with the following Coat of Arms:—ar. a fesse nebulée between three trefoils, slipped, gu., are these two epitaphs to the family of Thorpe, of Wanswell:—

"Here lyeth the body of MARY THORPE, second daughter of WILLIAM THORPE, Esq., who dyed February the 1ST, 1669, Aged 22."

"Here lyeth the body of GEORGE THORPE, Esq., who dyed July the 12th, 1672, Aged 32."

The lime trees were planted in the year 1753, by Thomas Clark.

The pillars and gates at the north entrance were erected in 1838, by Edwin Drinkwater Ghostley and Alfred Mayo, both natives of this parish.

This churchyard was closed for twenty years (vaults excepted) on 1st January, 1857. The last interment was on 31st December, 1856, viz:—

"MARGARET BROWNING, Widow, Berkeley, Aged 71."

The New Burial-Ground.

It was one of the wise practices of all ancient nations to dispose carefully of their dead. Some burnt them, that no mephitic vapours should arise to injure the living. By others, the art of preservation was carried to a high degree of perfection; while all such as buried their dead, were compelled by their laws to inter them without the gates of their towns and cities.

Among the Jews, fields seem generally to have been specially appropriated for this purpose. Abraham was buried with Sarah, his wife, in the cave of Macpelah, in the field of Ephron (Gen. xx. and xxiii.); and Uzziah, king of Judah, was buried with his fathers in the field which pertained to the kings (2 Chron xxvi.).

Among the early Christians, the burial of the dead outside the walls was emblematical of their passage from this world to their new kingdom of eternal joy.

The bad effects of burying within limited spaces in populous places is too notorious to be denied; and an annoyance being felt from the resting-place of our forefathers, it is a great source of congratulation that a new burying-ground has been formed here.

The piece of land added to the churchyard was given by the late Earl Fitzhardinge, but the walls, drainage, &c., &c., were executed at the expense of the parish. It was consecrated, though in an unfinished state, by the Right Rev. Charles Baring, D.D., Lord

Bishop of Gloucester and Bristol (translated to the See of Durham, 1861), on Friday, the 2nd day of January, 1857.

This ground not being ready, the dead were buried at Stone, near Berkeley, until February the 4th, on which day the first interment was made here, viz:—

"SWINBOURNE HADLEY, Purton, Aged 10 months."

BERKELEY BURIAL BOARD.

Notice is hereby given, that a meeting of the rate-payers of the parish of Berkeley will be held in the Vestry Room of the Parish Church of Berkeley, on Friday, the 6th day of February next, at 12 o'clock at noon, for the purpose of approving of the salary, wages, and allowances appointed for, and to be paid to the clerk, officers, and servants of the Burial Board for the said Parish of Berkeley, and for other special business connected with the said Burial Board.

William Smith,
Thomas Pearce, } *Churchwardens.*

Dated this 28th day of January, 1857.

THE TOWER.

The present tower stands at a distance of 146 feet from the church, on the north side of the churchyard, and occupies the same site as its predecessor. It was built in 1753, by Mr. Clark, at a cost of £740; and,

BERKELEY CHURCH TOWER.

to judge from an old picture in the Castle, it must be a fair imitation of the former one.

It is a square, massive, and venerable structure, and has open battlements and turrets. It is 76 feet 3 inches high, including the parapet which is in height 6 feet 6 inches; and 27 feet 10 inches wide at the base, including the buttresses, without them 20 feet 10 inches; but the parapet is 22 feet 11 inches wide.

It contains six bells, which bear the following inscriptions:—

I.—Rev. J. Seton-Karr, Vicar; T. Tratman, J. Alpass, J. Pick, R. Giles, C: Wardens. 1842. T. Mears, Fe.^{t.}

II.—The same.

IV.—The same.

III.—God save the King. Abra: Rudhall. 1700.

V.—Richard Palmer, Joseph Cole, George Bushell, William Burkcomb, Churchwardens. 1772. Abra. Rudhall, Bell founder.

VI.—Rev. Caleb Carrington, Vicar; John Rudhall, Glocester, Fec^{t.} 1808. Daniel Marklove, William Jones, William Ponting, Eli Gazard, Churchwardens.

Bells, in Popish times, were baptized, anointed, exorcised, and blest by the Bishop; whereupon the vulgar believed in their power to drive off the devil and evil spirits, to calm storms and tempests, and to perform numerous other prodigies. It was also common to give them the names of Saints, and to ornament them with verses.

The old custom of ringing the curfew-bell at eight

o'clock every night, from October 10th to March 25th, *yearly*, is kept up here.

The curfew-bell was so called because it was rung by a law of William the Conqueror, that all persons should then cover their lights and fires, and go to bed. Our Historians generally tell us that this Monarch was so jealous of the common people of England entering into cabals against his government, that he ordered all lights and fires to be extinguished in the houses upon the ringing of a certain bell, called the curfew-bell, suppressed by King Henry I. The ascribed imposition of the curfew custom, as a specimen of the Conqueror's rigid sway, merits but little credence. Thomson has thus described this supposed act of tyranny:—

> "The shiv'ring wretches, at the curfew sound,
>   Dejected sunk into their sordid beds,
>   And, through the mournful gleam of better times,
>   Mus'd sad, or dreamt of better."

Gray's Elegiac mention of the curfew is as familiar as "household words."

> "The curfew tolls the knell of parting day."

The clock was purchased and put up in 1765, and its face painted and gilded in 1783.

THE VICARAGE.

From an ancient terrier of the parish of Berkeley, bearing date the 9th of May, 1682, the Author has extracted the following entry:—

"Imprimis.—There is a vicarage-house, with a brew-house, and an orchard commonly called The Vicarage Close, containing between three or four acres, more or less; there are also four acres belonging to the Vicar, in a common meadow called Parham; also the herbage of the churchyard; the mounds of the churchyard to be kept in repair by the parish of Berkeley, the parish of Hill, and the Right Honourable the Earl of Berkeley, viz., the parish of Hill for the space of twenty-one yards; the Earl of Berkeley that part thereof next the Little Park; and the parish of Berkeley to maintain the residue of such mounds."

This vicarage is still standing; but is and has been for the last thirty-five years in a very dilapidated state, and in every way unsuited for the residence of a gentleman.

The Rev. John Seton-Karr, the vicar, for the last few years, has in consequence been obliged to reside in a house near the church, called Chantry Cottage, from its having once been the residence of the Chantry-priests.

In this vicarage-house Dr. Edward Jenner, the celebrated discoverer of vaccination, was born May 17, 1749.

His father was the Rev. Stephen Jenner, of Slimbridge, Rector of Rockhampton, and Vicar of Berkeley from 1729 till his death in December, 1754.

His mother was Sarah, daughter of the Rev. H. Head, Vicar of Berkeley from 1691 to 1728. She died in October, 1754.

Like every other discovery, vaccination was received with ridicule and contempt. Even religion and the Bible were made engines of attack against the doctor.

From these Errhman, of Frankfort, deduced his chief grounds of accusation against the new practice; and he gravely attempted to prove from quotations from the prophetical parts of Scripture, and the writings of the Fathers of the Church, that "Vaccination was the real Antichrist!"

The benefits which Jenner conferred upon mankind at last became universally admitted, and rendered his memory immortal.

In 1788, Dr. Jenner married Catherine, younger daughter of Robert Fitzhardinge Kingscote, Esq., of Kingscote, in this county; and about 1792 he took possession of Chantry Cottage above mentioned, where he died *suddenly*, January, 26, 1823, and was buried in the chancel of Berkeley Church. He left a son, Robert Fitzhardinge Jenner, Esq., who also died *suddenly* at Chantry Cottage, unmarried, and was buried in his father's vault, March 24, 1854; and a daughter, Catherine, who married Mr. Bedford, and, dying, left an only daughter, heiress to her grandfather.

MEMORANDA.

The following is a copy of an entry made in the churchwardens' book for the Tything of Ham:—

"April 4th, 1763.

It is agreed by, and with the consent of, the other two tythings, that the ten shillings a-piece, allowed by each tything for ringing, shall not be paid to the ringers, unless they ring, on the days appointed by payment, to the full satisfaction of the minister and churchwardens, and chime the vicar every Sunday to church, both mornings and evenings.

>HENRY KNOX.
>THOS. HICKES
>JOHN KING.
>RICHD. CROOME.
>JAMES PHILLIPS.
>NICHOLAS CORNOCK.
>WM. WADE.
>THOMAS WILTSHIRE.
>ROBERT PEARCE.
>JOHN JONES.
>JAMES WATTS.
>N. HICKES."

The following are copies of entries made in the churchwardens' book for the Tything of Alkington:—

"1765. To a new clock in the Tower, £5. 5s.
Robt. Clark's bill for putting up the same, £2. 15s.
Mr. Wm. Bennett, Churchwarden."

"Be it remembered, that in the night on 23rd of April, 1777, Berkeley Church was robbed of the Communion Plate to the value of sixty pounds.

And it was agreed some time after in the same year to purchase a sett of new Plate for the Communion, at the expence of the three Tythings.

The description of the new Plate bought in 1777:—

1 Large Flaggon, 1 Plate or Patten, 2 Fluted Gilt Cups. The whole cost £36. 17s. 4½d., and was all Engrav'd with this Inscription:—

Berkeley Communion Plate, 1777.

Joseph Sharp, Churchwarden, 1777."

"By cash for prosecuting Hugh Price, Chimney Sweeper, for stealing the Communion Plate out of the Parish Church of Berkeley and expences thereon, £11. 5s. 11d.

Robert Cole, Churchwarden, 1780."

"To one-third of a bill to William Joyner, for taking of Hugh Price and boy and William Smith for and on suspition of stealing the Communion Plate out of the Church, and attending the Assizes, £1. 1s.

To expences of the day, £1. 8s.

Robert Cole, Churchwarden, 1781."

"1783. Richd. Goodman for painting and gilding the face of the clock, £1. 1s.

Mr. Thomas Morse, Churchwarden."

HISTORY OF BERKELEY.

The number of Communicants at the Holy Communion at Berkeley and Stone in the reign of Edward VI. is given by the Royal Commission for Chantries, in the second year of his reign, in their report and certificate :—

The number at the church at Berkeley, one thousand one hundred and seventeen. At Stone Church, two hundred and thirteen.

A LIST OF SOME OF THE VICARS OF BERKELEY.

John Trevisa, of Cornwall, who translated the Bible into English at the request of Thomas Berkeley, fourth lord of that name, was presented to the vicarage of Berkeley by this lord. Trevisa died in the year 1409.

DATES.	INCUMBENTS.	PATRONS.
1575	John Norbrock.	Queen Elizabeth.
1586	William Green.	William Sprin.
1639	Thomas Tucker.	
	Edward Chetwynd.	
1668	Richard Saffin, M.A.	Chapter of Bristol.
	Jerome Gregory.	Earl of Berkeley.
1691	Henry Head, M.A.	Ditto.
1728	Ralph Webb, M.A.	Ditto.
1729	Stephen Jenner, M.A.	Ditto.
1755	George Chas. Black, M.A.	Ditto.
1758-9	Henry Knox, M.A.	Ditto.
1771-2	Augustus Thos. Hupsman.	Ditto.
1799-1800	Caleb Carrington.	Ditto.
1837	H. Prouse Jones, M.A.	Baron Segrave.
1839	John Seton-Karr, B.A.	Ditto.

BURIALS IN THE PARISH OF BERKELEY

OF PERSONS WHO DIED 80 YEARS OF AGE AND UPWARDS.

1813.

There were 43 burials in 1813.

Elizabeth Tratman, North Nibley, March 2, 81.
Mary Andrews, Berkeley, April 24, 80.
Mary Millard, Woodford, August 25, 82.
Giles Daniels, Berkeley, November 14, 81.

1814.

There were 38 burials in the year 1814.

Mary Wilts, Bevington, February 16, 84.
James Taylor, Wick, September 4, 82.

1815.

There were 41 burials in the year 1815.

Jane Denly, Alkington, November 24, 93.
Samuel Pegler, Berkeley, December 13, 83.

1816.

There were 40 burials in the year 1816.

Mary Ford, Ham, February 28, 90.
Hesther Purnell, Newport, May 15, 84.

1817.

There were 36 burials in the year 1817.

Josiah Fryar, Purton, March 13, 84.
Witsun Yearsley, Berkeley, October 26, 89.
Leonard Eding, Bevington, November 4, 80.

1818.

There were 66 burials in the year 1818.

Anthony Merret, Clapton, January 10, 81.
Hannah Ponting, Berkeley, June 9, 82.
Mary Latch, Wotton-under-Edge, September 27, 83.

1819.

There were 48 burials in the year 1819.

Anthony Wiltshire, Newport, January 20, 83.
Catherine Wood, Sugar Loaf, January 23, 92.
Sarah Latch, Berkeley, May 12, 83.

1820.

There were 58 burials in the year 1820.

Edward Curtis, Sanigar, January 26, 98.
Thomas Woolwright, Berkeley, March 3, 92.
Mary Browning, Pockington, March 20, 83.
Anne Cox, Berkeley, June 12, 84.

1821.

There were 49 burials in the year 1821.

Sarah Nicholas, Eastington, March 22, 89.

1822.

There were 48 burials in the year 1822.

Jane Nelms, Berkeley Heath, March 3, 82.
Hannah Smith, Berkeley, May 26, 80.

1823.

There were 53 burials in the year 1823.

Sarah Curtis, Sanigar, January 4, 90.
Betty Monday, Bevington, February 18, 88.
Ann Dorney, Halmore, June 17, 80.
Thomas Benett, Berkeley Heath, July 11, 85.
Mary Meddlemore, Berkeley, December 21, 84.

1824.

There were 52 burials in the year 1824.

Christian Pick, Bevington, January 6, 80.
Mary Barge, Alkington, May 12, 92.
Nathaniel Cook, Berkeley, July 11, 81.
Sarah Neale, Berkeley, August 7, 83.
Elizabeth King, Newport, September 16, 88.
Mary Woodbourne, Sanigar, September 18, 97.

1825.

There were 51 burials in the year 1825.

Sarah Cole, Ham, May 15, 80.
Mary Rickards, Wirewood Green, July 8, 82.

1826.

There were 68 burials in the year 1826.

Elizabeth Croome, Bush Street, September 10, 84.
Mary Marsh, Lorwinth, October 23, 88.
Thomas Baker, Berkeley, November 12, 82.
Anne King, Ham, December 22, 98.

1827.

There were 65 burials in the year 1827.

John Till, Bevington, February 27, 80.
William Cordy, Purton, June 4, 80.
John Tratman, Breadstone, July 11, 92.
Mary Longdun, Leather Bottle, November 23, 91.
John Griffin, Ham, December 13, 84.

1828.

There were 66 burials in the year 1828.

Mathew Church, Berkeley, March 10, 83.
Mary Pead, Ham, April 20, 91.
Rachael Croome, Newport, May 23, 82.
James Wickham, Berkeley, May 25, 84.
Mary Pearce, Berkeley, September 11, 90.
Anne Tanner, Ham, October 10, 82.

1829.

There were 63 burials in the year 1829.

Elizabeth Norman, Berkeley, January 28, 85.

Elizabeth Edwards, Newport, February 28, 80.
Thomas Merrett, the Park, March 28, 83.
Martha Spillman, Berkeley, April 5, 80.
Thomas Reynolds, Berkeley, April 16, 86.
Samuel Price, Alkington, May 28, 84.
Mary Cornock, Alkington, June 15, 81.
Abraham Gazard, Stock, August 28, 81.
James Cornock, Alkington, December 22, 82.

1830.

There were 60 burials in the year 1830.

Thomas Gabb, Lorwinth, January 8, 86.
Mary Price, Bevington, January 24, 84.
Mary Millard, Bevington, January 24, 86.
Nathaniel Browning, Woodford, February 10, 81.
William Pain, Berkeley, March 14, 85.
Mary Malpas, Berkeley Heath, April 4, 92.
Anne Pick, Ham, April 25, 82.
Mary Brown, Michaelwood, July 12, 87.
Thomas Carpenter, Newport, July 18, 82.
Deborah Haviland, Sharpness Point, July 25, 82.
Sarah Watts, the Park, December 16, 92.
Elizabeth Hupsman, Berkeley, December 31, 89.

1831.

There were 57 burials in the year 1831.

Joseph Page, Newport, February 19, 80.
Jane Merrett, Berkeley, May 22, 82.

Betty Merrett, Berkeley, June 15, 80.
James Pearce, Ham, August 1, 81.
Edward Wynne, Bevington, September 8, 82.
John Dennis, Newport, December 25, 88.

1832.

There were 58 burials in the year 1832.
Ann Smith, Berkeley, July 11, 86.
John Crump, Weatenhurst, July 24, 87.
Ann Humphries, Berkeley, November 8, 80.
Mary Howell, Hinton, December 17, 87.
Anthony Kingscott, Halmore, December 30, 86.

1833.

There were 72 burials in the year 1833.
William Cornock, Blanchworth, January 2, 83.
Mary Andrews, Brown's Mill, January 31, 87.
Elizabeth Griffin, Clapton, June 16, 86.

1834.

There were 58 burials in the year 1834.
Daniel Marklove, Berkeley, January 27, 82.
James Phillips, Ham, February 12, 82.
Lydia Kitheroe, Woodford, March 2, 85.
Sarah Creese, Purton, March 15, 90.
Sarah Cornock, Aust, June 5, 86.
Mary Price, Berkeley, June 12, 81.
Sarah Jackson, Halmore, December 21, 80.
William Tiley, Ham, December 21, 80.

1835.

There were 55 burials in the year 1835.

Elizabeth Caston, Sanigar, February 10, 81.
Betty King, Berkeley, March 10, 91.
Hannah Lewis, Ham, June 9, 93.
Anthony Stone, Berkeley, November 1, 80.
William Tanner, Ham, December 22, 80.

1836.

There were 57 burials in the year 1836.

John Parslow, Berkeley, February 4, 80.
William Ricketts, Woodford, March 15, 82.
Robert Glastonbury, Berkeley, November 9, 84.
Sarah Gabb, Cam, December 9, 88.
Catherine Norman, Berkeley, December 30, 88.

1837.

There were 71 burials in the year 1837.

Rose Cornock, Cockshut, January 5, 82.
Sarah Jones, Berkeley, January 8, 87.
Edward Cook, Wanswell, January 10, 80.
Richard Barrett, Bevington, March 19, 85.
John Butts, Berkeley, June 26, 83.

1838.

There were 59 burials in the year 1838.

Daniel Lewis, Ham, January 16, 85.
Elizabeth Mason, Newport, March 1, 84.

Mary Luce, Berkeley, March 4, 83.
James Hinder, Halmore, April 1, 84.
William Williams, Crossways, August 16, 80.
Thomas Hood, Berkeley, August 31, 83.
William Mann, Berkeley Heath, September 20, 86.
George Hughes, Clapton, September 26, 86.
Sarah Smith, Berkeley, November 7, 86.
Ann Phillips, Thornbury, December 21, 88.

1839.

There were 66 burials in the year 1839.

Betty Cornock, Blanchworth, March 2, 80.
Ann Taylor, Berkeley, May 10, 83.
Mary Gainer, Swanley, September 7, 88.
Robert Humphries, Berkeley, September 26, 85.

1840.

There were 75 burials in the year 1840.

Sarah Haines, Mobley, March 13, 80.
Job Dimery, Wanswell, March 18, 80.
Sarah Joyner-Ellis, Berkeley, April 11, 95.
Mary Hill, Breadstone, April 15, 97.
William Arthurs, Thornbury Union, May 19, 80.
Thomas Tuck, Michaelwood, May 23, 80.
Elizabeth Tuck, St. Michael's Wood, June 26, 80.
Anne Alpass, Wanswell, September 2, 88.

End of First Book.

Burials from Second Register Book for Berkeley.

1841.

There were 68 burials in the year 1841.

Robert Norman, Berkeley, January 5, 85.
Elizabeth Purnell, Berkeley, January 27, 86.
Nicholas Jones, Berkeley, January 29, 85.
Mary Hale, Heathfield, June 20, 82.
Sarah Barge, Ham, December 10, 80.

1842.

There were 49 burials in the year 1842.

Sarah Thayer, Butler's Farm, January 24, 81.
Hester Heaven, Newport, May 1, 88.
Thomas Hickes, Berkeley, July 23, 92.

1843.

There were 66 burials in the year 1843.

Betty Dowall, Berkeley, January 15, 88.
Hannah Nash, Bevington, January 19, 82.
Martha Wicks, Woodford, February 23, 81.
Sally Croome, Breadstone, March 21, 93.
Ann Palser, Thornbury Union, August 18, 80.
Rhoda Phillpott, Berkeley, December 6, 82.
Susanna Fryer, Hinton, December 13, 82.
Thomas Workman, Thornbury Union, December 22, 88.

1844.

There were 86 burials in the year 1844.

Ann Fryer, Brookend, February 2, 84.
Sarah Cole, Stone, February 28, 84.
Samuel Workman, Thornbury Union, February 28, 80.
Mary Summers, Berkeley Heath, March 12, 82.
Elizabeth Smith, Framilode, May 22, 89.
Sarah Mason, St. Michaelwood, August 7, 82.
Thomas Merrett, Purton, August 12, 86.
Henry Lewis, Woodford, September 21, 83.
Thomas Hinder, Berkeley Heath, October 18, 84.
Anne Williams, Berkeley, October 26, 84.
Mary Watts, Ham, December 12, 89.

1845.

There were 51 burials in the year 1845.

Thomas Yearsley, Thornbury Union, January 9, 90.
Molly James, Ham, April 7, 84.
Joshua Ball, Hinton, September 9, 85.
James Lane, Newport, December 28, 85.

1846.

There were 49 burials in the year 1846.

Ann Wilks, Newport, March 8, 86.
Solomon Philpot, Berkeley, April 28, 82.
Thomas Pearce, Ham, June 4, 88.
Mary Smith, World's End Farm, July 4, 82.
James Mallett, Berkeley, September 2, 96.
Sarah Parslow, Berkeley, November 14, 84.

1847.

There were 64 burials in the year 1847.

Elizabeth Knight, Berkeley, January 29, 84.
Sarah Beaven, Berkeley, January 31, 92.
Mary Bence, Berkeley Heath, February 7, 85.
Thomas Neale, Berkeley, March 19, 80.
Ashfield Shipway, Heathfield, March 21, 99.
Betty Stone, Halmore, May 13, 84.
Anne Hughes, Clapton, June 27, 85.
George Williams, Berkeley, July 24, 84.
Samuel Greening, Berkeley, September 24, 84.
George Charrett, Thornbury Union, November 21, 84.

1848.

There were 71 burials in the year 1848.

James Phillips, Wanswell, March 9, 83.
Samuel Munday, Ham, June 7, 83.
Mary Ruell, Berkeley, June 23, 82.
Hannah Dix, Berkeley, July 11, 82.
Sarah Williams, Berkeley, August 17, 90.
George Gazard, Wick, September 22, 86.

1849.

There were 81 burials in the year 1849.

Hannah Allen, Ham, January 30, 82.

Ann King, Lynch, February 1, 85.
Susannah Hulbert, Clapton, Feb. 28, 90.
Edward Canston, Newport, March 4, 84.
Esther Kingscote, Ham, March 31, 85.
Ann Hinder, Berkeley Heath, May 11, 94.
Phœbe Butt, Berkeley, May 24, 86.
John Mills, Clapton, June 12, 88.
Hester Merrett, Ham, June 22, 90.
Robert Allen, Ham, July 12, 87.

1850.

There were 66 burials in the year 1850.

Hester Hill, Berkeley, January 16, 94.
Hannah Gainer, Cam, February 3, 95.
Susan Poole, Berkeley, April 4, 91.
William Jenkins, Woodford, April 5, 80.
Sarah Price, Stock, April 24, 86.
Daniel Deane, Dursley, April 25, 89.
John Creed, Berkeley, June 16, 81.
Mary Payne, Thornbury Union, October 7, 80.
Mary Long, Mobley, November 9, 87.
Ann Mundy, Berkeley Heath, December 10, 80.

1851.

There were 60 burials in the year 1851.

Lydia Sanigar, Blackhole, July 7, 81.
Sarah Mallett, Berkeley, August 1, 96.

1852.

There were 50 burials in the year 1852.

Elizabeth Dimery, Hogsdown, January 8, 84.
James Grafton, Thornbury Union, Feb. 26, 80.
Daniel Ruther, Ham, March 3, 87.
John Pick, Vine Farm, June 7, 100.
Sophia Taylor, Wick, December, 11, 82.

1853.

There were 68 burials in the year 1853.

William Smith, Berkeley, March 10, 90.
Thomas Gale, Wanswell, April 3, 92.
Daniel Nelms, Berkeley Heath, June 5, 84.
Rhoda Perkins, Woodford, July 13, 80.
Thomas Alpass, Wanswell, December 3, 97.
Deborah Lewis, Berkeley, December 25, 86.

1854.

There were 43 burials in the year 1854.

Hannah Bishop, Ham, July 27, 84.
Jonah Munday, Clapton, September 17, 83.
Thomas Smith, Halmore, September 18, 82.
Hannah Croker, Breadstone, September 27, 86.
Richard Browning, Halmore, December 10, 84.

1855.

There were 80 burials in the year 1855.

Ann Daw, Crawless, February 21, 81.
Naomi Hopkins, Berkeley, May 20, 80.
Betty Franklin, Ham, May 30, 87.
Henry Matthews, Wanswell, August 4, 82.
Jonah Woodward, Halmore, December 6, 89.

1856.

There were 54 burials in the year 1856.

Thomas Griffiths, Berkeley, March 24, 85.
Tracey Bow, Thornbury Union, June 30, 82.

1857.

There were 64 burials in the year 1857.

Mary Woolright, Berkeley, January 12, 85.
Hannah Harris, Woodford, April 23, 80.
Hannah Wilkins, Woodford, June 30, 80.
Samuel Harris, Stone, September 13, 83.
Ann Trotman, Berkeley, October 18, 85.
Sarah Bennett, Berkeley, Nov. 15, 84.
Elizabeth Humphreys, Ham, December 6, 83.

1858.

There were 54 burials in the year 1858.

John Taylor, Wanswell, January 13, 81.
Hester Ruther, Wanswell, March 10, 92.
Ann Ruther, Mobley, March 12, 83.
Mary Prewett, Berkeley, March 16, 85.
William Humphreys, Ham, May 5, 81.
Frances Matthews, Wanswell, September 12, 82.

1859.

There were 50 burials in the year 1859.

George Dash, Ham, March 20, 85.
Ann Mundy, Blissbury, August 4, 86.
Hester Webb, Purton, November 30, 99.

1860.

There were 67 burials in the year 1860.

Robert Ruther, Berkeley, January 3, 84.
William Reynolds, Berkeley, February 3, 82.
Sarah Powell, Halmore, February 13, 81.
Elizabeth Eddle, Sanigar, March 14, 82.
John Powell, Halmore, April 9, 89.
James Tucker Ghostley, Berkeley, July 11, 86.
William Mundy, Berkeley Heath, November 30, 89.
George Bennett, Stock, December 25, 87.

1861.

There were 40 burials in the year 1861.

Anne Pearce, Berkeley, January 19, 82.
Hester Kemmett, Halmore, January 27, 87.
Sarah Nash, Thornbury Union, February 25, 80.
Mary Reynolds, Berkeley, March 16, 83.
Sarah Eddle, Wanswell, June 11, 82.
John Oldland, Woodford, June 22, 85.
Sarah Woodward, Halmore, July 19, 95.
Anne Screen, Woodford, September 1, 90.

1862.

There were 56 burials in the year 1862.

John Barton, Newport, January 17, 85.
Mary Taylor, Wanswell, February 14, 80.
Christopher Gazard, Thornbury Union, February 18, 84.
Betty Bow, Thornbury Union, May 20, 85.
Richard Cornock, Berkeley, June 22, 80.
Alice Millard, Purton, July 24, 86.
Prudence Lawrence, Kitts Green, August 4, 87.
Samuel Grafton, Halmore, October 9, 87.
Sarah Ballinger, Heathfield, October 15, 86.
Hester Cornock, Berkeley, October 26, 81.
Hannah Smith, Wanswell, November 29, 89.
Lois Lawrence, Berkeley, December 25, 81.

1863.

There were 56 burials in the year 1863.

Giles Powell, Hinton, February 9, 82.
Richard Spillman, Stock, March 6, 81.
Hannah Michell, Berkeley Heath, March 25, 85.
William Cooper, Berkeley, June 20, 85.
John Pick, Peddington, November 10, 82.

* The earliest Register Books begin January 8, 1813, previous to that date the books are in the House of Lords.

BERKELEY CASTLE —— View from the Meadows.

Chapter IV.

THE CASTLE.

> "This castle hath a pleasant seat; the air
> Nimbly and sweetly recommends itself
> Unto our gentle senses."
>
> *Macbeth, Act I., Scene VI.*

Rudder says, "The castle was begun in the 17th year of King Henry the First, by Roger de Berkeley (the second), and finished by Roger the third in the reign of King Stephen."

The Saxon Chronicle (p. 223) states, that "King Henry the First was at Berkeley in the Easter of 1121;" four years after the foundation of the castle.

From Dugdale the Author finds that this Roger was barbarously and perfidiously used by Walter, brother of Milo, Earl of Hereford, and violently ejected out of his castle at Berkeley.

It is apparent from these evidences that there was a castle here in the reign of King Henry the First.

Mr. Smyth, who wrote "The Lives of the Berkeleys," was of opinion that there was not one *here*, but that Dursley was meant, where there was a castle before the Conquest, the residence of these Berkeleys. This Author, referring to a deed in the castle, says: —"In the southest end of the towne is seated the castell of Berkeley, a great part whereof was built out of the ruines of the Nunnery, which stood in the same place, which was demolished by the practise of Earle Godwin, in the time of Edward the Confessor. The buildinge of this castell was by King Henry the Seconde, in the time of King Stephen, while the said Henry was Duke of Normandy, as plainly appears by a deed of the said Duke Henry's, made to Robert, the sonne of Harding, wherein the duke dothe acknowledge to have covenanted with the said Robert to build for him there a castle, accordinge to the will of the said Robert; and then gave his oathe to perform the same; as did also nyne other noblemen with the duke. And to see this building the better performed, the said Duke Henry, not long before the deathe of King Stephen, came in person to Berkeley. Howbeit, it is certain that, at this first building, the castle contained no more than the inmost of the three gates, and the buildinges within the same; for the two utmost gates, and all the buildings belonging unto them, save the Keepe, were the additions of Lord Maurice, eldest sonne of the Lord Robert, in the latter end of King Henry Second, and of Lord Thomas, the seconde of

that name, in Edward II., and of Lord Thomas, the third of that name, in Edward III."

From this account it appears that the present castle was undoubtedly founded the latter end of the reign of King Stephen.

The reader must judge for himself whether there was a castle here before or not. The fact of the Berkeleys having a castle at Dursley is no reason why they should not have had another at Berkeley. Indeed, the Author thinks it very possible that, owing to the civil wars between the Empress Maude and Stephen, Roger de Berkeley did erect a castle here, however small, and that it was demolished by Henry II., when he deprived this Roger of his Barony and Manor, and gave them to his opulent friend, Robert Fitzharding. At all events, the *original* portion of the present castle was founded by Henry, Duke of Normandy, who came in 1154 to superintend its construction.

It is a fine structure of the feudal times, and one of the few buildings of that period which is still preserved from ruins. It stands on a rising eminence, and overlooks an extensive surface of rich and level pasture land. The battlements command a more extended view: the eye ranges over a large tract of open, flat country, thickly ornamented with rich woodland, and bounded by distant hills, and the river Severn, of which latter there is a beautiful prospect.

A delightful view is obtained of Stinchcombe, Nibley, and Wotton hills, Tortworth Court, and the Monu-

ment at Hawkesbury Upton. The Wyndcliff on the Wye, and the Forest of Dean are also seen.

Its *present* form approaches nearest to that of a circle, and the buildings are enclosed by an irregular courtyard, a dry moat, and terrace, with a straight bowling-green.

It appears that the *original* castle in Robert Fitzharding's time consisted of the Keep, and the Gateway which joins it. After passing through this Gateway, the Keep *was*, and *is*, approached by a sidelong flight of steps, over which is the Guard-room, *now* called King Edward's Room. At the top of the steps, on the left, is the grand doorway—a fine Norman arch, and said to be a remnant of the Nunnery. Proceeding through this archway to the south, the visitor arrives at the Dungeon Tower,* in which is the Dungeon Chamber, and underneath it the Dungeon, which is twenty-eight feet deep. Southward is another tower, called The Lady's Hold. Westward is a tower, called Thorpe's. The fourth, or Northern Tower, *formerly* a chapel, is now the Muniment or Evidence Room, where the documents of the family are kept. The Kitchen was in the wall, with a strong external abut-

---

* Dungeon—Fr. *Dongeon, ou Donjon*—a dungeon, the strongest tower or place in a castle, where prisoners were wont to be kept.

Prisoners being usually confined in these strong towers, the word *dongeon* was applied to other strong close places of confinement or imprisonment. *Dongeon* is used by Chaucer:—

"I salued her, and enquired what she was, and why she, so worthie to sight, dained to enter into so foule a *dongeon*, and namely a prison, without leaue of my keepers."—*Chaucer.* "*The Testament of Loue,*" b. i.

BERKELEY CASTLE—THE KEEP.

ment on the outside. The Keep *was* roofed in by leads, *now* uncovered: it has evidently undergone great alterations.

At the present day the interior of the Keep is a grass-plat; and in the wall on the south side there is a large opening, no doubt the demolition of the Civil Wars in 1645, for the purpose of rendering the castle, then a place of residence, defenceless. About 1255, Maurice, Lord Berkeley, beautified the east, south, and west, with walks and gardens.

In 1326 and 1327, Thomas, fifth Lord Berkeley, enlarged the Castle; and in 1344 and 1345, this Lord built that part outside the Keep on the north-east side, adjoining the great kitchen, and gave to the castle its present circular form.

In the sixteenth century, Henry, Lord Berkeley, built the stone bridge to the *first* entrance, where before was a drawbridge of timber.

This entrance leads into the outer court, where the Keep and Thorpe's Tower present a very imposing appearance.

There is another entrance, on the north, into this court, over a stone bridge, now disused: it leads into the adjoining park.

The *second* entrance-gate defends the Inner Court, and joins the Keep: here are the residence of the Lord, and the apartments of his retainers. In this gateway, the groove of one portcullis is visible.

> "There stands the castle, by yon tuft of trees,"
>
> *Richard II., Act II., Scene III.,*

said our great Bard upwards of two centuries and a half ago, and the Author questions if it has changed in appearance one *iota* since that time.

The Dining-Room,

(*In the late Earl's time the Hall.*)

This is lofty and capacious, and was built in the reign of Edward the Third. It has been the scene of revelry and feudal pomp. It is 32½ feet in height, 62 feet long, and 32 feet wide.*

It has undergone no alteration of importance since the late Earl's death beyond the erection (by the present Lord) of a handsome carved oak screen across the lower end. It is now warmed by flues, furnished, carpeted, and used as a Dining-room by the family.

On one of the tables lies a Russian musket, taken at the Battle of Inkerman by Lieutenant (now Major) Maxse, a nephew of Lord Fitzhardinge, who greatly distinguished himself in the late war.

At one end is the accustomed dais, elevated above

---

* The writer of an article in the *Leisure Hour*, Part XVI., April, but published May 2, 1853, No. 66, p. 245, has very erroneously stated the Hall to be "more than 90 feet long and 30 wide."

The Author, in the year 1856, measured the Hall himself, and he has *recently* had it measured, which measurement agrees with his own, so that the reader must receive the above account as the correct one.

the floor, and a very antique fireplace. At the opposite end, facing the dais, is a small gallery, formerly used by the musicians, and behind it a pointed window of modern insertion, which reaches to the roof. The walls are decorated with swords, banners, figures in ancient armour, bucklers, cross-bows, and matchlocks.

> "Let me wander in the Hall,
> Round whose antique visag'd wall
> Hangs the armour *Britons* wore,
> Rudely cast in days of yore."

There are four windows, of modern introduction, looking into the inner court, which extend to the commencement of the roof, containing a well-executed series of heraldic shields, emblazoned with the alliances of the Berkeleys for many generations.

On the opposite side there are two windows looking on the terrace: there *were* three, but the third is stopped up.

THE DRAWING-ROOM,

(In the late Earl's time the Dining-Room.)

This room is spacious, and wainscoated with fine oak panels.

A couch of ebony, which formerly belonged to the celebrated Sir Francis Drake is here, but his bedstead and chairs of the same wood are in another part of the castle.

The walls are covered with full-length portraits of the Berkeley family, and others, with one of Queen Elizabeth, let into the paneling. There is a fine copy of Rubens' "Tribute-Money," over an elaborate fireplace.

In one corner is a recess, being part of a small tower, in which is a collection of scarce and antique china. In it was placed, a few years ago, the silver-framed mirror and silver toilet equipage service which formerly belonged to Queen Elizabeth. They were brought from Cranford, and came into possession of the Berkeleys from Lord Hunsdon, whose daughter, Elizabeth Carey, married Lord Berkeley.

This room is *now* used with the two next rooms, which were in the *late* Earl's time the Drawing-room and Music-room, as a suite of Drawing-rooms.

The second Drawing-room is very elegantly and tastefully furnished. In it there is a beautiful old cabinet, inlaid with tortoiseshell; some very beautiful pictures and family portraits.

The Chapel.

This chapel was built in the reign of Edward the Third.

Its windows, narrow and stained, are set in the thickness of the wall, and overlook the terrace.

The roof is of wood, painted black, and supported by corbels, which are in excellent preservation.

On the altar stands a small marble *relievo* of a Roman sacrifice.

On one side of it is a low-legged carved chair, said to have belonged to Queen Anne.

In front of it stands a lectern—a large bronze eagle, supporting on its back and wings a black-letter Prayer-book and Bible, bearing date 1633 and 1640.

At the opposite end of the chapel, raised considerably above the floor, is the gallery for the family.

This chapel is used for family prayers.

The Chalice, or Godwin Cup.

Mr. Marklove, in his "Views of Berkeley Castle," gives the following account of this cup, but does not state whence he obtained his information:—

"This was a favourite cup of Earl Godwin's, from which, on every morning, he used to quaff; but, as the legend runs, he neglected once his usual custom, and on that day the sea swallowed up the chief of his estates, now known as the Godwin Sands. May the Lord prosper us."

The truth is, the Godwin Sands were formerly part of the estate of the famous Earl Godwin; but, through neglect of keeping the walls, &c., in repair, the sea overflowed them about the end of the reign of William Rufus, or the beginning of that of Henry the First.

This is an elegant and elaborately embossed silver cup, and is gilt with gold.

On the top of the cover outside, under the ball and cross, are emblazoned the Royal Arms of James the First.

THE CHALICE, OR GODWIN CUP.

Inside the cover is engraved :—

"Earl Godwin, anno 1066.—New gilt for the present Earl of Berkeley's coming of age, anno 1766."

The former part of this inscription is evidently an error, since Earl Godwin died in the year 1053.

In the bottom of the cup are the Arms of Berkeley.

King Edward's Room.

"Mark the year, and mark the night,
When Severn shall re-echo with affright,
The shrieks of death through Berkeley's roofs that ring;
Shrieks of an agonizing king."

Gray's Bard.

This castle has been the scene of various remarkable transactions; the most melancholy of which was the barbarous murder of Edward the Second, in 1327.

When the death of this unfortunate sovereign had been resolved on by the Queen, and Mortimer (her infamous paramour), he was removed to Berkeley Castle, and committed to the custody of Thomas, third Lord Berkeley. Owing to the humanity with which this Lord treated the captive Monarch, he was soon after obliged to relinquish his castle and prisoner to Lord Maltravers and Sir Thomas Gourney, by whom the king was soon afterwards murdered, through the wicked subtlety of Adam de Orleton, Bishop of Hereford, who wrote unto his keepers these few words, without points between them:—"*Edwardum occidere nolite timere bonum est:*" that, by reason of their different sense and construction, both they might commit the murder, and he also excuse himself.

These enigmatical words have been thus translated:—

"To murder King Edward fear; not to do it is praiseworthy."
"To murder King Edward fear not; to do it is praiseworthy."

And again:—

"To seek to shed King Edward's blood.
Refuse to fear I think it good."

This last sense the Bishop desired his words might be understood in, as indeed they were.

Thomas de la More, who was Privy Councillor to Edward, and wrote his life, says that the murder was committed with a plumber's iron:—"*Cum ferro plumberri intense ignito,*" &c.—P. 603.

Walsingham, in his history, says:—"*Ipso prostrato, et sub ostio ponderoso detento ne surgeret, dum tortores imponerent cornu in ano suo (quod dictu verecundum est) et per foramen immitterent ignitum veru in viscera sua.*"—Page 127.

And Holinshed says:—"His crie did move many within the castell and town of Birckelei to compassion, plainly hearing him utter a waileful noyse, as the tormenters were about to murder him: so that dyvers being awakened thereby (as they themselves confessed), prayed heartilie to God to receyve his soule, when they understode by his crie what the matter ment."

The sufferings this poor Monarch went through, and the indignities he suffered, may have been in the

mind of Shakespeare, when he wrote that melancholy passage placed in the mouth of a similar sufferer, Richard II.:—

> "Let us sit upon the ground,
> And tell sad stories of the death of kings."
> *Richard II., Act III., Scene II.*

After his death, Abbot Thokey had the courage to go, attended by his brethren, solemnly robed, and accompanied by a procession from the City of Gloucester, and claimed the body for burial, which, with the observance of all possible respect, he conveyed in his own chariot, *drawn by stags*, to the Abbey, where it was buried with becoming solemnity.

The south aisle of this Cathedral Church, was rebuilt by the offerings which devout people made at the shrine of King Edward II., which were so large, that the Register of the Abbey says, "If they had been all expended on the church, they might have built it from the ground;" so great a respect was paid to the memory of that injured prince.

The Choir of this Cathedral was also built out of the pious offerings to his remains; and the votaries to his shrine, for some time after his death, could hardly find room in the city, so great was the concourse.

A small apartment, called Edward's Room, over the steps leading to the Keep, is pointed out as the room where this dire cruelty was perpetrated. At that time all the light it received was from arrow-slits: the

windows have been since introduced. A plaster cast of the king's bust kept here is taken from his effigy on the tomb in Gloucester Cathedral; and what is shown as the implement of torture, is evidently nothing more than an old fencing-foil.

It is advanced by the late Mr. Shrapnell, and by the Rev. T. D. Fosbroke, "that the murder was committed in the Dungeon-room; and that, to annoy and distress the captive, his keepers put putrid carcases and other nuisances in the dungeon underneath; and the unfortunate king bitterly complained of it at the window to some carpenters at work upon the castle." History, unfortunately, does not inform us of the room in which the murder was committed; and Antiquarians are not agreed upon the subject, whether it took place in Edward's Room, or the Dungeon-room.

The Author would observe here, that the king being a state prisoner—Lord Berkeley being allowed £5 a-day for his expenses—would have the castle for his prison, and not be confined to *one* apartment. It was customary at this early period to make prisons of the gate-houses, and for the state prisoners to occupy the apartments over them.

It is, therefore, probable that Edward occupied the apartments over the second entrance, and was murdered there, from whence it is more likely his screams would be heard by the townspeople than if he had been murdered in the Dungeon-room or Guard-room.

After the murder, Lord Berkeley was arraigned as a

participator in the foul deed, but was honourably acquitted by his Peers of being accessory to Edward's death.

THE LADY'S HOLD.

This is the portion of the castle to which the females retired for safety; it consists of chamber above chamber, the upper one opening on the leads over the second entrance or gateway.

Here was the promenade of the ladies, and occasionally of the state prisoners.—*Wharton's Poetry*, III., 13.

THORPE'S TOWER,

Now the Flag Tower, is called from a family of the name of Thorpe (*long since extinct*) who held their estate at Wanswell, in this parish, by the tenure of guarding it. This estate is *now* the property of Lord Fitzhardinge. This tenure has a parallel in the case of Staunton Tower,* in Belvoir Castle, Leicestershire, which is held by the representative of the family of Staunton, of Staunton, Nottinghamshire.

* Burke, in his "Landed Gentry," says,—"There is an ancient custom, when any of the Royal family honour Belvoir Castle with their presence, for the chief of the Staunton family personally to appear and present the key of the stronghold of the castle (called Staunton's Tower) to the Royal visitors."

In 1342, this tower, then in ruins, was rebuilt by Thomas, Lord Berkeley. From its summit, when Lord Fitzhardinge is at home, waves the flag on which are emblazoned the Arms, Crest, Supporters, and Motto of the family.

Nothing more of moment occurs till the Civil Wars.

During these wars, Berkeley Castle was besieged several times, and surrendered to Cromwell's forces in 1645.

In the *Bibliotheca Gloucestrensis*, by John Corbett, it is recorded:—"Sept. 23, 1645. Berkeley Castle was now the only considerable fortress between Gloucester and Bristol that contained a royal garrison, and Colonel Rainsborough was sent by Fairfax to reduce it. He arrived before it on the twenty-third of September, and sent in a summons.

Sir Charles Lucas, the Governor, returned for answer that he would eat horse-flesh before he would yield, and man's flesh when that was done; and to a second summons he gave as peremptory a reply.

Then the assailants applied their scaling-ladders against the Church and outworks, and stormed them. Forty men were slain, and ninety taken prisoners.

And when the Governor saw that the main strength of the place was lost, and that the besiegers were planting their ordnance against him from his own works which commanded the castle, he sounded a

parley, and commissioners were sent out to treat of a surrender.

The Castle of Berkeley was yielded upon these articles :—

That the Governor should march out with three horses and his arms, and not above £50 in money; every field-officer, with two horses and but £7 in money; foot captains, with swords, but no horse; common soldiers, without arms, and not above 5s a-piece.

Five hundred horse and foot marched out of the gate; and eleven pieces of ordnance, and six months' provisions fell into the hands of the captors."

The castle, however, was shortly restored to the Lord of Berkeley with the *proviso*, that it was to remain in a defenceless state.

The castle and town have suffered much from time to time through the incursions and sieges to which they were exposed.

"There is something," says Whitaker, "in the nature of all privations which exposes them to be burlesqued;" and accordingly a Poet, who was not in love with hardships, has hit upon this very circumstance :—

> "In days of old our fathers went to war,
> Expecting sturdy blows and hardy fare;
> Their beef they often in their murrions stew'd,
> And in their basket-hilts their beverage brew'd."

Thus much for the castle: and now the Author

resigns the Visitor into the hands of the Housekeeper, who shows this Baronial residence, which has stood seven hundred years; and concludes by borrowing the expression of Bacon:—

"It is a pleasing thing to see an ancient castle or building not in decay, or to see a fair timber tree sound and perfect: how much more to behold an ancient family which hath stood against the waves and weathers of time!"

Chapter V.

THE BERKELEY FAMILY.

As the pedigree of this noble house is in every Peerage, it will be unnecessary to give it here. The Author will, however, make the reader acquainted with the *Founder of the Barony*, and also lay before him some *Memoirs* of those personages who have shone conspicuously in the annals of history, not recorded in those works.

History relates that an ordinance was made in Denmark that, if the King of that land had more sons than one, the eldest should succeed his father on the throne, and the younger ones should be sent into other countries.

Thus it happened that

HARDING, second son of the King of Denmark, was sent into England to King William the Conqueror, unto whom this King gave great riches, and sent him to Bristol to live there in the year 1069.

He was Mayor and Governor of that city, and,

dying, was buried there 16 Henry I., 1116; and was succeeded by

Robert Fitzharding, his eldest son and heir.

He was likewise Mayor and Governor of Bristol; and in 1140 he began the foundation of the Abbey of St. Augustine's there, which he dedicated and endowed April 11, 1148; and afterwards became a Canon therein. He, firmly adhering to Maud, the Empress, and her son Henry, Duke of Normandy (afterwards King Henry II.), whom he assisted with great supplies of money in their wars against King Stephen, had (in remuneration of his fidelity, and services done unto them, in their great contests with King Stephen) from the said Duke, on coming to the throne, the whole Lordship of Berkeley, and all that territory thereabouts called Berkeley-Herness; of which lordship and territory, Roger de Berkeley, owner of Dursley, was then divested.

The grant of Berkeley-Herness was made between September 7, 1150, and October 25, 1154. The Hundred of Berkeley was appendant to the Manor.

The *tenure was* by Barony, and Lord Berkeley took his place and precedence from the first year of Henry II., anno 1154.

This Robert Fitzharding took part with, and entertained at Bristol, in 1168, Dermot Mac Murrough, King of Leinster, with sixty of his adherents, who then solicited succours from Henry II. to assist him in recovering his kingdom, from which he had been expelled by

the kings of Meath and Connaught; by means thereof in 1172 King Henry took possession of Ireland.

He died 5 February, 1170-71, aged 75; buried in St. Augustine's; and was succeeded by his eldest surviving son,

MAURICE DE BERKELEY.

He was the *first* who dwelt at Berkeley, and took the name, and dropped that of Harding.

He gave 1,000 marks to King Henry II. for confirmation of the grant of Berkeley and Berkeley-Herness.

He fortified the castle, and took in part of the Churchyard, for which the Abbot of St. Augustine's prosecuted him with Church censures.

He founded two hospitals; viz., Lorrenge, between Berkeley and Dursley, and Longbridge, at the northern entrance into Berkeley.

In fact, so benevolent were the early members of this family, that Smyth, in his "Lives of the Berkeleys," asserts, an assertion corroborated by Fuller, "that they have been the greatest benefactors to the Church of the whole Nobility of England—no less than eighty Knights' fees being held of them by religious houses; nor is there scarcely a church in this county, or even in adjacent counties, where the Arms in the windows do not denote a benefaction. The family have, on this account, an Abbot's mitre for a crest."

This Lord died 16th June, 1190, and was buried at Brentford, near London, to which church he had been

a great benefactor. He was succeeded by his eldest son,

ROBERT DE BERKELEY.

He went with King John to the wars in France.

He and the rest of the Nobles having been much oppressed by this King demanding large sums of money of them for renewing charters, escuage, and other services, took up arms against him, and thereby incurred his Majesty's displeasure, but soon after recovered the Royal favour. Again falling from his allegiance, the Castle of Berkeley and all his lands were seized by the King: only the Manor of Cam was allowed for his wife's maintenance.

Henry III. succeeding to the crown, he sued for pardon, and had all his estates restored to him, *except* the town and castle of Berkeley, by paying a fine of £966 and 1 mark, 1 Henry III., to the Earl of Pembroke, Earl Marshal of England, and Protector of the young King.

He dying 13th May, 1220, without issue, about 55 years of age; buried in St. Augustine's; was succeeded by his brother,

THOMAS DE BERKELEY.

He complied with the King's will, and had Berkeley Castle and town restored to him, 8 Henry III., 1223.

He died 29th November, 1243, aged 76; buried in St. Augustine's; and was succeeded by his eldest son,

MAURICE DE BERKELEY.

This Nobleman, before the death of his father, was

two years with King Henry III. in the wars in France.

He entertained this King at Berkeley Castle in July, 1256, on his return from Bristol, where he had been on a visit of four days to his son Prince Edward; and in return for his kindness, Henry III. pardoned this Lord and his tenants their breaches of Assize in merchandize and measure, belonging to the King as Supreme Clerk of the Market, and forgave him his taxes held anciently from Manors of the Demesnes of the Crown. He accompanied his Majesty against the Welsh in 42, 43, and 44 Henry III. He served sixteen times in person in the King's wars; but he afterwards adhered to the rebellious Barons, for which insurrection against the King his lands were seized by the Crown. He obtained pardon of the King in 1271.

He died 4th April, 1281, seized of the Barony of Berkeley, which he held by the service of three Knights' fees, and was buried in St. Augustine's. He was succeeded by his eldest surviving son,

THOMAS DE BERKELEY.

He was with the King at the siege of Kenilworth Castle, in October, 1266; and he was afterwards in the Welsh wars; for which eminent services he had a special grant, *temp. Edward I.*, of liberty to hunt the fox, hare, badger, and wild cat, with his own dogs, in the King's forests of Mendip and Chase of Kingswood, except *in mense vetito*, fence time.

His amusements were tournays, hawking, hunting, and agriculture at home.

He was at the battle of Evesham, where Simon de Montfort, the great Earl of Leicester, was slain; he was engaged in the French wars in 25 Edward I.; he shared in the victory of Falkirk, gained 22nd July, 1298; he was at the celebrated siege of Kaerlaverok, in 1300; and, lastly, he was taken prisoner at the fatal battle of Bannockburn, June 24, 1314, but afterwards obtained his freedom by paying a large fine. He went into the wars twenty-eight times.

He was summoned to Parliament as a *Baron* by *Writ*, from 23rd June, 1295, to 15th May, 1321.

This great warrior died 23rd July, 1321, aged 76, seized of the Castle and Hundred of Berkeley; buried in St. Augustine's; and was succeeded by his eldest son,

MAURICE DE BERKELEY, second Lord, who had summons to Parliament, *as Lord Berkeley, of Berkeley Castle*, from 6th August, 1308, to 15th May, 1321.

Being of a military disposition in his youth, he was in several tournaments in England; and was in all the Welsh, Scotch, and French wars with his father.

His Lordship was made Governor of Gloucester in 1312; the King committed to him the custody of the town and castle of Berwick-upon-Tweed in 1314; he was made Justice of South Wales in 1315, and had the keeping of all the castles there; and in 1319 he was made High-Steward of the Duchy of Aquitaine, and a Baron in his father's lifetime. On his return from

Aquitaine, he joined with Thomas Plantagenet, Earl of Lancaster, and other Lords, against the Spencers, and laid waste all their estates, and caused them to be banished; but the Spencers were recalled within a year by an Act of Parliament, and their opponents declared traitors.

This Lord was consequently, in 1321, committed prisoner to Wallingford Castle, and all his estates were forfeited. He died there 31st May, 1326, aged 45, but was buried in St. Augustine's, and was succeeded by his eldest son,

THOMAS, third Lord, who was summoned to Parliament from 14th June, 1329, to 20th November, 1360.

To this Nobleman the custody of the unhappy Edward II. was committed, and whose melancholy death is related in page 79.

This Lord had restitution of his lands, 1 Edward III., which had been forfeited by his father joining in rebellion with Thomas, Earl of Lancaster; and he had Berkeley Castle restored to him when the Queen's army marched from Gloucester that way.

This Lord was always in arms on all the King's expeditions: he was at the battle of Cressy, in 1346, with Edward III.; at the taking of Calais, 31st December, 1348; and at the battle of Poictiers,* won

* The following anecdote is extracted from Froissart's account of the battle of Poictiers:—"It happened that, in the midst of the general pursuit, a squire from Picardy, named John de Helennes, had quitted the

19th September, 1356, where the King of France was taken prisoner. He was, in short, twenty-two times, in the reign of Edward III., in wars with the French, or Welsh, or Scotch.

king's division, and, meeting his page with a fresh horse, had mounted him, and made off as fast as he could. At that time, there was near to him the Lord of Berkeley, a young knight, who, for the first time, had that day displayed his banner: he immediately set out in pursuit of him. When the Lord Berkeley had followed him for some little time, John de Helennes turned about, put his sword under his arm in the manner of a lance, and thus advanced upon the Lord Berkeley, who taking his sword by the handle, flourished it, and lifted up his arm in order to strike the squire as he passed. John de Helennes, seeing the intended stroke, avoided it, but did not miss his own; for as they passed each other, by a blow on the arm he made Lord Berkeley's sword fall to the ground. When the knight found that he had lost his sword, and that the squire had his, he dismounted, and made for the place where his sword lay; but he could not get there before the squire gave him a violent thrust which passed through both his thighs, so that, not being able to help himself, he fell to the ground. John upon this dismounted, and, seizing the sword of the knight, advanced up to him and asked if he were willing to surrender. The knight required his name: 'I am called John de Helennes,' said he; 'what is your name?' 'In truth, companion,' replied the knight, 'my name is Thomas, and I am Lord of Berkeley, a very handsome castle, situated on the river Severn, on the borders of Wales.' 'Lord of Berkeley,' said the squire, 'you shall be my prisoner: I will place you in safety, and take care you are healed, for you appear to me to be badly wounded.' The knight answered, 'I surrender myself willingly, for you have loyally conquered me.' He gave him his word that he would be his prisoner, rescued or not. John then drew his sword out of the knight's thighs, and the wounds remained open; but he bound them up tightly, and, placing him on his horse, led him a foot-pace to Châtel-Herault. He continued there, out of friendship to him, for fifteen days, and had medicines administered to him. When the knight was a little recovered, he had him placed in a litter, and conducted him safe to his house in Picardy, where he remained more than a year before he was quite cured, though he continued lame; and when he departed, he paid for his ransom six thousand nobles, so that this squire became a knight by the great profit he got from the Lord of Berkeley."—*Vol. II., chap.* 160.

His piety was as eminent as his valour, for he founded several chantries:—Amongst which, in 17 Edward III., he founded a Chantry in the Chapel of St. Maurice, at Newport, near Berkeley, endowing it with divers lands and rents in Berkeley, Wotton, and Alkington. He also gave to the Chantry-priest of our Lady, in the Church of Berkeley, and to his successors, divers lands in Ham, to hold an Anniversary on the day of Petronilla the Virgin, for the Lord Maurice his father, in Berkeley Church; as also for Margaret his mother; and for himself after his decease.

His Lordship died 27th October, 1361; buried in Berkeley Church; and was succeeded by his eldest son, by his first wife,

MAURICE, fourth Lord, who was born about the end of the fourth year of Edward III.

In 11 Edward III., being then but seven years of age, he was taken into Scotland, by his father, and there knighted, to prevent wardship; and the year following, though but eight years old, married Elizabeth, the daughter of Hugh le Despenser.

This Sir Maurice went to Granada when fourteen years old, and stayed abroad two years. He attended the Black Prince into Gascony, and was badly wounded and taken prisoner at the celebrated battle of Poictiers.

The Earl of Salisbury obtained leave for this Lord to come to England; and the King gave his patent, February 12th, for him to come over and return by

the 20th day after Michaelmas; and he did return, but paid for his ransom £1,080 of English money sterling.—*MS. Veel*, page 389.

He died June 8, 1368, aged 37; buried in St. Augustine's; and was succeeded by his eldest son,

THOMAS, fifth Lord, being then fifteen years old.

He was a great soldier, both by land and sea, having been in all the wars in France, Scotland, and Wales. In 1403 he was made Admiral, when Charles the Sixth of France sent forces to Glendowrdwy, and they arrived at Milford Haven, where he burnt fifteen sail of their ships, and took fourteen, on board of which was the Seneschal of France, and eight officers of note, whom he made prisoners.

He entertained King Richard II. at Berkeley Castle in 1387.

He was a great lover of learning, and an especial favourer of that worthy person, John Trevisa, Vicar of Berkeley, in his time; of whom Bale gives this character, that he was *vir multâ eruditione atque eloquentiâ clarus*. Which John, moreover, was a Canon of the Collegiate Church of Westbury, Wilts, and translated into English the Old and New Testaments at his request.

This Lord dying 13th July, 1417, without male issue, was succeeded by his nephew,

JAMES, sixth Lord, the only surviving son of James, who was brother to the last Lord (Thomas).

In consequence of the large estate concerned, a lawsuit was carried on between this Lord and his pos-

terity with his cousin Elizabeth, heiress of the last Lord (Thomas), and her posterity, which lasted 192 years. This feud was carried on with great violence, and much bloodshed ensued. Amongst some of the transactions, the following occurred:—"In 18 Henry V., one David Woodburne, with divers others of his fellow-servants of their master, John Talbot, Viscount Lisle, coming to Wotton, served this Lord James with a *subpœna* for his appearance in the Chancery, and insisted on obeying the process. This Lord James not only beat the parties, but 'will he nill he' inforced the said David to eat the *subpœna*, wax, and parchment."— *MS. Berkeley*, page 488.

This Lord died 22nd October, 1463; buried in Berkeley Church, and was succeeded by his eldest son,

WILLIAM, seventh Lord.

He was created Viscount Berkeley 21st April, 1481; advanced to the dignity of Earl of Nottingham in 1483; and created Marquess of Berkeley 28th January, 1489.

This Nobleman carried on the lawsuit with his cousin Thomas Talbot, Viscount Lisle, concerning some lands claimed by the latter in right of his grandmother, Margaret, Countess of Shrewsbury, the granddaughter of Thomas, Lord Berkeley, who died 13th July, 1417. This variance rose to such a height, that they fought the celebrated battle of Nibley Green, in 1469, wherein Viscount Lisle was slain, being shot with an arrow through the mouth *as his beaver was up*.

This Marquess died 14th February, 1491, and, leaving no issue, his own honours (which he had purchased of King Henry VII. and his courtiers, by settling his castle and lands upon them) ceased; but the Barony of Berkeley should have passed to his brother Maurice, had not the Marquess, in anger with him for not marrying a person of honourable parentage, settled the Castle of Berkeley and the lands belonging to that ancient Barony, upon King Henry VII., and the heirs male of his body, in failure of which to descend to his own right heirs. In consequence of this conveyance, his brother,

MAURICE (eighth Baron by right) enjoyed none of the estates, and was entirely deprived of the Peerage. This Maurice, however, obtained his share of an estate which devolved upon him in right of his mother.

He lived at Thornbury, and dying in 1506, aged 71; buried in Friers Augustine, London; was succeeded by his eldest son,

MAURICE (ninth Baron by right), who was brought up at Thornbury.

He went abroad, and became a great soldier.

When he was in England he resided at Yate, and styled himself Maurice Berkeley, Esq.; but when he was in the King's service he styled himself Maurice Berkeley, son and heir of Maurice Berkeley, Lord Berkeley. He was made a Knight of the Bath at the coronation of King Henry VIII.

This Sir Maurice died September 12, 1524, aged

57, at Calais, and was buried there; and, leaving no issue, was succeeded by his brother,

THOMAS (tenth Baron by right), who was likewise educated at Thornbury.

He was Captain over a body of men at the celebrated battle of Flodden Field, fought 9th September, 1513, and for his signal service was Knighted in the field by the General, Thomas Howard, Earl of Surrey.

This Sir Thomas died 22nd January 1532, aged 60, and was *first* buried at Mangotsfield, but *afterwards* removed to the new tomb which he had erected in the Abbey Church of St. Augustine's, Bristol; and was succeeded by his son,

THOMAS (eleventh Baron by right), who was brought up at St. Omer's, France.

He died at Stone, near Dartford, Kent, 19th September, 1535, aged 29; was buried there, and was succeeded by his posthumous son,

HENRY (twelfth Baron by right), who, upon the death of King Edward VI. (the last male heir of Henry VII.), succeeded as heir to Berkeley Castle and lands, which had been settled upon Henry and his heirs male by the Marquess of Berkeley.

His Lordship was summoned to Parliament by Queen Mary in right of the ancient Barony of the family.

This Lord died 26th November, 1613; buried in Berkeley Church; and was succeeded by his grandson and heir,

GEORGE, thirteenth Baron, K.B., and son of Thomas, who died before his father.

He died 10th August, 1658, and was succeeded by his only surviving son,

GEORGE, fourteenth Baron, who was created, 11th September, 1679, Baron Mowbray, Segrave, and Breaus, Viscount Dursley, and Earl of Berkeley.

This Nobleman was one of the Committee of Lords and Commons sent to the Hague, in May, 1660, by both Houses of Parliament, to present their humble invitation and supplication, " that his Majesty would be pleased to return, and take the government of the kingdom into his hands; where he should find all possible affection, duty, and obedience, from all his subjects."—*Clarendon's History of the Civil Wars*, Vol. III., Book xvi., p. 600.

" They presented from the Parliament £50,000 to his Majesty, to defray his debts with; £10,000 to the Duke of York, and £5,000 to the Duke of Gloucester, for their several necessities; as presents from them."—*Clarendon*, Vol. III., p. 600.

"The King embarked for England May 24, landed at Dover May 26, and entered London May 29,* 1660 (the anniversary of his birthday), in a most splendid and

---

* Although Charles II. did not become King *de facto* until the 29th of May, 1660, his regnal years were computed from the death of his father, 30th January, 1649; so that the year of his restoration is called the *twelfth* of his reign. This was done under an opinion of the Judges, who resolved, that from the instant of his father's death, though excluded from the kingly office, he was King both *de jure* and *de facto*.

magnificent manner, and was then solemnly proclaimed King."—*Clarendon*, Vol. III., p. 602. Edition of 1704. Oxford.

This Lord was in great favour with the Duke of York, and together with his nephew Charles, had the principal management of his Royal Highness's family.

He was also a member of the Privy Council in the reigns of Charles II., James II., and William III.*

This Lord died 14th October, 1698, and was succeeded by his eldest son,

CHARLES, fifteenth Baron and second Earl, K.B.

He was summoned to the House of Peers as Baron Berkeley, of Berkeley, 11th July, 1689.

His Lordship died 24th September, 1710, and was succeeded by his second, but eldest surviving, son,

JAMES, sixteenth Baron and third Earl.

He was summoned to Parliament, 7th March, 1704, by the title of Lord Dursley.

He was a distinguished Naval Officer during the reign of Queen Anne. In Sir George Rooke's engagement with the French fleet off Malaga, 13th August, 1704, he commanded the *Boyne* of eighty guns. In

---

* He was Author of a little book, valuable for its merit as well as its rarity, entitled "Historical Applications and Occasional Meditations upon several subjects. 1670, 12mo."

"In this book are several striking instances of the testimony which some men have borne to the importance of a religious life, and the consolation to be received from it, especially at the approach of death."—*Granger's Biog. Hist.*, Vol. III., p. 212.

The above work was reprinted in 1838, by C. Richards, St. Martin's Lane, London.

August 1707, his Lordship, riding at anchor before one of the Isles of Hieres, in which were three forts, surprised the strongest, and summoned the two others, which surrendered at discretion.

This Lord was succeeded at his decease in 1736 by his only son,

AUGUSTUS, seventeenth Baron and fourth Earl, K.T.

His Lordship likewise distinguished himself as a Military Officer, and obtained the command of one of the regiments embodied to march against the Scotch and English rebels in 1745, and the Pretender's army was defeated at Culloden, 16th April, 1746.

He died 9th January, 1755, aged 39; and was succeeded by his eldest son,

FREDERICK-AUGUSTUS, eighteenth[*] Baron and fifth Earl.

This Nobleman was constituted Lord-Lieutenant and Custos-Rotulorum of the County of Gloucester, and of the Cities of Gloucester and Bristol, Constable of the Castle of St. Briavel, and Warden of the Forest of Dean; also Keeper of the Deer and Woods in the said Forest;[†] and High-Steward of Gloucester.

---

[*] The writer of an article in the *Saturday Magazine* for July 23, 1836, Vol. IX., p. 26, states that, this Earl is *two-and-twentieth* in descent from Robert Fitzharding, first Lord of Berkeley. That writer reckoned the descent from the feudal tenure of Berkeley Castle, since the time of Henry II.; whereas the Author of this work reckons from the creation by writ, June 23, 1295.

[†] Of *forests* and *woods* (fallow deer), Fuller thus writes:—

"The deer therein, when living, raise the stomachs of gentlemen with their sport; and, when dead, allay them again with their flesh. The fat

He died 8th August, 1810, aged 65; was buried in the Sepulchral Chapel adjoining the Chancel of Berkeley Church; and his eldest son,

WILLIAM-FITZHARDINGE BERKELEY, succeeded to the Castle and Manor of Berkeley.

He presented a petition to the Crown for a Writ of Summons as Earl Berkeley, but the House of Lords in 1811 came to a resolution that the petitioner had not substantiated his claim.

He was created Baron Segrave in 1831, and Earl Fitzhardinge in 1841.

His Lordship was Lord-Lieutenant and Custos-Rotulorum of Gloucestershire, and Colonel of the South Gloucester Militia.

He died unmarried, October 10, 1857, aged 70, and was buried in the Sepulchral Chapel aforesaid. On his demise, his brother,

SIR MAURICE-FREDERICK-FITZHARDINGE BERKELEY,

---

of venison is conceived to be (but I would not have deer-stealers hear it) of all flesh the most vigorous nourishment, especially if attended with that essential addition which Virgil coupleth therewith—.

'*Implentur veteris Bacchi, pinguisque ferinae,*'

(Old wine did their thirst allay, fat venison hunger).

—*Fuller's Worthies*, p. 325, Edit. 1662.

Again, he says:—

"But deer are daily diminished in *England*, since the gentry are necessitated into thrift, and forced to turn their pleasure into profit, *Jam seges est ubi Parcus erat;* and since the sale of *bucks* hath become ordinary, I believe, in process of time, the *best stored park* will be found in a *cook's shop* in London."—*Fuller*, p. 325.

G.C.B., succeeded to the Castle* and Manor of Berkeley.

He presented a petition to the House of Lords, July 12, 1860, claiming the honour and dignity of Baron of Berkeley, and after several lengthy hearings of this claim the Attorney-General concluded thus, "Under all the circumstances, he must say that, in his opinion, the claimant had not made out his case. Their Lordships then adjourned the further consideration *sine die*."—*The Times*, August 13, 1860.

He was created Baron Fitzhardinge, August 5, 1861.

His Lordship is a Privy Councillor, an Admiral, and a Magistrate for Gloucestershire.

*** THOMAS - MORETON - FITZHARDINGE BERKELEY, fifth son of the fifth Earl, *de jure* present Earl of Berkeley, but he does not assume the title.

The Author having now finished his collection of some of the *Memoirs* of this illustrious family, thinks he

---

* On Wednesday, 15th February, 1860, the Prince of Orange paid a visit to this ancient structure. A troop of the South Gloucestershire Hussars escorted his Royal Highness from Stone, and on reaching the Castle the band of the Royal South Gloucester Militia played the national Dutch anthem. The Prince was received by Sir Maurice and Lady Charlotte Berkeley, and the party staying at the Castle—Lady Emily and Miss Ponsonby, Lord William Lennox, Colonel and Mrs. Berkeley, and Mrs. Charles Berkeley—were presented to him. After visiting the building a handsome lunch was prepared in the grand hall, and on taking his departure the heir to the throne of Holland expressed his high gratification at the reception he had met with.

cannot do better than take leave with the words of Scott:—

> "Names known too well in Scotland's war,
> At Falkirk, Methven, and Dunbar,
> Blazed broader yet, in after years,
> At Cressy red and fell Poictiers."
>
> *Lord of the Isles, Canto VI., 25.*

Chapter VI.

THE FREE SCHOOL, BRIDEWELL HOUSE, ETC.

The Free School.

This school was endowed by Samuel Thurner, Esq., of Thornbury, in this county, Bachelor of Physic of Magdalen Hall, Oxford. By his last Will and Testament, dated October 5th, 1696, he gave certain lands in the parishes of Berkeley, Rockhampton, and Thornbury, for the educating of poor boys and girls of this town. In the year 1856, there were twenty-six boys and five girls. There were also twelve other boys—three of the town, and three of each tything—educated in this school by the endowment of John Smith, A.M., of Magdalen College, Oxford, in the year 1717.

The house on Canonbury-hill, formerly used for this school, was the property of Lord Fitzhardinge, who pulled it down in 1861, and a School-house was erected in that year, opposite the Vicarage Close.

This house is in the hands of Trustees for the use of the school, and no rent is paid for it.

There are not any girls educated in it *now*, but about thirty-six boys.

Lady Fitzhardinge's Schools.

These schools (adjoining the Wesleyan Chapel) were built in 1861 by Lord Fitzhardinge, by whom they are supported, and more than 200 children receive a good and plain education.

The Bridewell House.

This house was given by an unknown Benefactor for the benefit of the poor of this town. It formerly consisted of tenements, the rental of which from 1683 to 1813 varied from six to twenty pounds a-year.

Being in ruins and uninhabited, it was pulled down in 1856, and a very good house built on the site by the *late* Earl Fitzhardinge, in which a branch of the National Provincial Bank of England was established in 1862.

The Town House.

This house was likewise given by an unknown Benefactor for the benefit of the poor of this town. It is still inhabited, the rental of which goes to the poor.

The Market House.

This is a good and substantial stone building, and was built in the year 1824. It was not built on the site of the old Market House, but nearly opposite to where it stood. It is apparent from Domesday-book, that there was a market held in this town in the time of Edward the Confessor, and also of William the Conqueror. A grant, however, was obtained by Robert, son of Robert Fitzharding, of King Henry II., in the first year of his reign, to hold a market here every Tuesday: this has been discontinued for many years.

This Market House is now used for the monthly market, the first Wednesday in every month, established in 1859, for the sale of cheese, butter, &c.

The room above it (called the Town Hall) is used daily by the British School and Young Men's Society. Occasionally concerts, &c., are held here.

The Police Station.

A *new* Police Station was erected in 1861, in Canonbury Street, opposite the Post Office. This is a handsome building, and quite an ornament to the town.

Petty Sessions are held *here* now, instead of *where* they used to be, viz., at the *White Hart Inn*.

TRADE.

The clothiers' business was an important one here *formerly*, but it ceased about forty-eight years ago. The cheese business was also carried on to some extent, but this likewise terminated about the same period. The trade *now* is in tanning, malt, timber, and coal.

A LIST OF SOME OF THE MAYORS OF BERKELEY,

collected from documents in the Town Chest from 1625 to 1727 inclusive, and from the Court Leet Rolls, in the Castle, from 1750 to 1855 inclusive.

NAMES.	YEARS.	NAMES.	YEARS.
WILLIAM HALE	1625	JOHN CLARKE	1638
	1626		1639
	1627	EDMUND ———	1640
THOMAS WALKER	1628		1641
	1629	JOHN WALKER	1642
	1630		1643
THOMAS MARLIM	1631	JAMES ROBERTS	1644
WILLIAM HALE	1632		1645
CHARLES JAY	1633	WILLIAM SMITH	1646
	1634	FERDINANDO SHAWE	1647
WILLIAM LAURENCE	1635	JOHN EDWARDS	1648
	1636	JOSEPH ATKINES	1649
WILLIAM HAWKINS	1637	JOSIAS EDMONDS	1650

NAMES.	YEARS.	NAMES.	YEARS.
Clemwell Woodward	1651	Cornelius Lawrence	1693
Thomas Pearce	1652	Daniell Clarke	1694
Thomas Pearce	1653	George Lewis	1695
Charles Smyth	1654	George Lewis	1696
Thomas Nelme	1655	William Neale	1697
Richard Tratman	1656	James Baily	1698
Robert Eswate	1657	John Barker	1699
Thomas Laurence	1658	John Barker	1700
Thomas Pearce	1659	Cornelius Lawrence	1701
David Pretchett	1660	John Vick	1702
Richard Pallmer	1661	John Tyler	1703
Henrye Lewes	1662	William Beaven	1704
John Morris	1663	Arthur Beaven	1705
Thomas Pearce	1664	James Watts	1706
John Smyth	1665	Edward Lucas	1707
Daniell Crome	1666	Daniell Clarke	1708
John Collins	1667	Daniell Clarke	1709
	1668	Daniell Packer	1710
Daniell Crome	1669	Thomas Dening	1711
	1670	Obadiah Laughaine	1712
John Nelme	1671	Obadiah Laughaine	1713
	1672	Thomas Varnham	1714
Samuel Cowle	1673	Thomas Varnham	1715
Thomas Laurence	1674	John Bayly	1716
Thomas Laurence	1675	Mr. Bayly	1717
Maurice Attwood	1676	John Pick	1718
Nathaniell Laurence	1677	William Raymond	1719
Thomas Beavan	1678	William Raymond	1720
	1679	Richard Palmer	1721
	1680	William Warner	1722
	1681	William Hooper	1723
	1682	Thomas Dening	1724
John Somers	1683	James Beaven	1725
John Pallmer	1684	Robert Marklow	1726
Joseph Tyler	1685	Obadiah Laughaine	1727
Joseph Tyler	1686		1728
Mr. Somers	1687		1729
Mr. Cambridge	1688		1730
Nathaniel Gardner	1689		1731
Nathaniel Lawrence	1690		1732
Nathaniel Lawrence	1691		1733
John Smyth	1692		1734

HISTORY OF BERKELEY. 111

NAMES.	YEARS.	NAMES.	YEARS.
	1735	William Parslow	1777
	1736	Thomas Woolright	1778
	1737	Wm. Lawrence Parslow	1779
	1738	John King	1780
	1739	William Neale	1781
	1740	Jonathan Halling	1782
	1741	William Spillman	1783
	1742	John Summers	1784
	1743	Wm. Lawrence Parslow	1785
	1744	James Prewatt	1786
	1745	William Joyner	1787
	1746	William Grafton	1788
	1747	Daniel Marklove	1789
	1748	James Russell	1790
	1749	John Hopkins	1791
Mr. Samuel Stoke	1750	Thomas Pearce	1792
Richard Smith	1751	John Bick	1793
Robert Marklove	1752	John Summers	1794
Robert Lloyd	1753	William Joyner	1795
Henry Somers	1754	William Grafton	1796
Alexander Raymond	1755	John Marklove	1797
John Laugharne	1756	Thos. Woolright, Jun.	1798
Nicholas Hickes	1757	Henry Jenner	1799
Nicholas Hickes	1758	Thomas Neale	1800
Thomas Pearce	1759	John Halling	1801
William King	1760	Thomas Hickes	1802
Samuel Parker	1761	Edward Jenner, M.D.	1803
James Prewatt	1762	James Simmons	1804
Benjamin Cotten	1763	Daniel Marklove	1805
Thomas Gwinn	1764	Viscount Dudley	1806
William Turner	1765	Robert Pearce	1807
William Parslow	1766	Thos. Woolright, Jun.	1808
Thomas Woolright	1767	Henry Jenner	1809
John Parslow	1768	John Phillips	1810
Richard Smith	1769	Thomas Neale	1811
John King	1770	John Halling, S. N.	1812
William Neale	1771	M. F. F. Berkeley, Captain R.N.	1813
Jonathan Halling	1772		
Alexander Raymond	1773	Thomas Hickes	1814
William Spillman	1774	George Smith	1815
Benjamin Cotten	1775	J. H. B. Morgan	1816
Thomas Gwinn	1776	Edward Jenner, M.D.	1817

NAMES.	YEARS.	NAMES.	YEARS.
Robert Pearce	1818	John Thorn	1841
M. F. F. Berkeley, R.N.	1819	Thomas Woolright	1842
R. Fitzhardinge Jenner	1820	Francis Hands	1843
William Duberly	1821	Francis Hands	1844
Robert Norman	1822	E. Drinkwater Ghostley	1845
Timothy Tratman	1823	William Pope	1846
Henry Marklove	1824	William Pope	1847
Charles Marklove	1825	William Smith	1848
George Smith	1826	Stephen Alpass	1849
James Gastrell Phillips	1827	Daniel Sutton	1850
John Spier	1828	John Cox Hickes	1851
John Spier	1829	David Legge	1852
George Smith	1830	William Gaisford	1853
William Day	1831	Thomas Adams	1854
George Seaborn	1832	Thomas Woolright	1855
John H. B. Morgan	1833	Francis Hands	1856
Daniel Sutton	1834	E. D. Ghostley	1857
John Cox Hickes	1835	John Cary	1858
R. Fitzhardinge Jenner	1836	Col. F. W. F. Berkeley	1859
Robert Norman	1837	William Pope	1860
James Drake	1838	William Pope	1861
Timothy Tratman	1839	J. G. Phillips	1862
James Gastrell Phillips	1840	D. Sutton	1863

Note.—No record exists of the names not given.

Chapter VII.

THE WITCH OF BERKELEY.

The "Berkeley Witch" of William of Malmesbury lived in the time of Edward the Confessor. She was so wicked, that the fiends are reported to have run away with her body from Berkeley Church in the presence of the Clerks singing for her soul! The following legend was applied to this place, which shall be given in faithful translation from William of Malmesbury, who seems to have been the original authority, and he had the story from an eye witness. "When I shall have related it," he says, "the credit of the narrative will not be shaken, though the minds of the hearers should be incredulous, for I have heard it from a man of such character, *who would swear he had seen it*, that I should blush to disbelieve." — *Sharpe's William of Malmesbury*, p. 264.

"A woman used to reside in Berkeley, accustomed, as it afterwards appeared, to crimes, not ignorant of the ancient auguries, a patroness of the palate, arbitress of petulance, putting no moderation to her sins, because

she was as yet on this side of old age, although beating on the door of it with a near foot. When this woman was on a certain day holding a feast, a raven, which she kept as a pet, croaked something louder than usual.

Upon hearing this, the knife fell from her hand, her countenance became pale, and groaning, she exclaimed, 'To day my plough has come to its last furrow; to day I shall hear and receive a great misfortune.' While speaking the words, the messenger of miseries entered.

Being asked why he came with a face so full of expression, 'I bring news to you,' he said, 'from that town,' and named the place, 'of the death of your son, and destruction of all the family, by a sudden ruin.'

At these words, the woman, wounded in her mind with grief, immediately swooned away, and feeling the disease creep to her vitals, invited her surviving children, a monk and nun, with speedy letters, and addressed them upon their arrival, with a sobbing voice. 'I, my children, by my miserable fate, have always used demoniac arts; I have been the sink of all vices, the mistress of enticements. There was, however, among these evils, a hope of your religion, which might sooth my miserable soul. Despairing of myself, I reclined upon you; I proposed you to be my defenders against demons, protectors against the most cruel enemies. Now, therefore, because I have reached the end of my life, and shall have those exactors of the punishment whom I had advisers in my sin, I ask you, by the maternal bosom which you have sucked, if you have

any faith, any piety, that you at least attempt to alleviate my sufferings; and though you will not recall the sentence issued concerning my soul, yet perhaps you will preserve my body by this means. Sew it in a stag's hide, afterwards recline it in a stone sarcophagus, fasten the cover with lead and iron; besides this, surround the stone with three iron chains, viz.—of great weight; let there be psalm-singers for fifty nights, and the same number of masses in the days, which may mitigate the ferocious attacks of my enemies. So, if I should lie securely for three nights, on the fourth day bury your mother in the ground, although I fear that the earth, which I have so often burdened with my vices, will not receive me in her bosom.'

Her desires were complied with in the most attentive form.

But oh! her wickedness: pious tears, vows, prayers, availed nothing; so great was the wickedness of the woman, so great was the violence of the Devil.

For, on the first two nights, when choirs of clerks were singing psalms around the body, certain devils, breaking with the greatest ease the door of the church fastened with a huge bolt, burst asunder the two chains at the extremities. The middle one, which was more elaborately wrought, remained entire.

On the third night, about cock-crowing, the whole monastery seemed to be overturned from its foundations by the noise of the approaching enemies. One more terrible than the rest in look, and taller in stature,

shaking the doors with greater force, dashed them into fragments.

The clerks stood stiff with terror, their hair on end, and bereft of speech. He advancing with a proud step to the coffin, and calling the woman by name, ordered her to arise.

Upon her answering that she could not on account of the chains, 'You shall be loosed,' said he, 'and to your evil;' and immediately broke the chain, which had eluded the ferocity of the rest, with as much ease as packthread. He also kicked off the lid of the coffin with his foot, and having taken her by the hand, drew her out of the church in the sight of them all.

Before the doors stood a proud black horse neighing, with iron hooks projecting over his whole back.

The woman was put upon it, and soon disappeared from the eyes of the spectators, with the whole company.

The cries of the woman, supplicating for help, were heard for nearly four miles."

SCRIPTOR. P. BED. 48.

*** Inventions like these were common modes of revenge among Ecclesiastics, a similar story being told of the body of Charles Martell, King of France, and others.

Perhaps the farce was acted by persons in disguise, for this was also usual. At all events, the woman had bitter enemies, and was so traduced upon the same grounds as the vulgar slander the memory of deceased persons whom they dislike, by affirming (to use their own language) that "*they walk;*" a calumnious custom, derived from this ancient practice.

THE END.

NOTICES OF THE PRESS ON THE FIRST EDITION.

"This is a carefully and correctly compiled history of this ancient town, with its castle and church. The old place is full of interest—teems, as it were, with narrative and tradition, and Mr. Fisher has done ample justice to his subject. We recommend the work to our readers."—*Bristol Times, July 26, 1856.*

"By the aid of modern facilities of transit, by land and water, there are so many persons now constantly visiting the town of Berkeley, that we are sure this brief history will be considered a great acquisition by the curious traveller. It is carefully and correctly compiled, and confers credit upon the author, the Rev. J. Fisher."—*Gloucester Journal, August 2, 1856.*

"A charming little hand-book, giving a description and history of the town of Berkeley, its castle and church, compiled by the Rev. John Fisher, curate of that place, has just been published, and no doubt will prove an acceptable companion to all who may be led to visit a spot which is so fruitful in time-honoured associations. Mr. Fisher has aimed, in his guide, both at perspicuity and conciseness, and has fully succeeded. The book, which is illustrated by some good engravings, is dedicated to the Earl Fitzhardinge."—*Cheltenham Journal, August 9, 1856.*

Lightning Source UK Ltd.
Milton Keynes UK
171878UK00005B/42/P